Jeremy Soul

Daytime Dating

Never Sleep Alone

Daytime Dating - Never Sleep Alone   by Jeremy Soul

Published by Classic Books Publishing, Christoph Lymbersky, Luetkensallee 41, 22041 Hamburg. Classic Books Publishing is a label of the MLP Management Laboratory Press UG, registered in Hamburg, Germany.

Copyright © 2010 by Love Systems Inc.

Disclaimer:

All rights reserved. No part of this publication may be reproduced or distributed in any form or by any means, or stored in a database or retrieval system, without the prior written consent of Love Systems Inc., including but not limited to, in any network or other electronic storage or transmission, or broadcast for distance learning.
This work is not to be considered professional, medical, psychological or legal advice. It is for entertainment purposes only. Love Systems, Inc., or our associates, or affiliates will not be liable for any direct or indirect consequences that occur from the use of any of the ideas contained this book.

Publication date: October 2010, Hamburg, Germany

Registered with:
ISBN-Agentur für die Bundesrepublik Deutschland in der MVB Marketing- und Verlagsservice des Buchhandels GmbH
Bibliografische Information der Deutschen Nationalbibliothek:
Die Deutsche Nationalbibliothek verzeichnet diese Publikation in der Deutschen Nationalbibliografie; detaillierte bibliografische Daten sind im Internet über http://dnb.d-nb.de abrufbar.

Front Cover Picture: © Classic Books Publishing & Love Systems Inc.
Interior Pictures: : © Love Systems Inc.
Text Layout: : © Classic Books Publishing

When ordering this title, use ISBN: 3941579711
the EAN-13 is 9783941579712

DAYTIME DATING: Never Sleep Alone

Table of Contents

Preface 13

Introduction 17

Acknowledgements 19

Magic Bullets 21
    Differences in Daytime Dating... 21
    Caveats 23

How to use this book 25
    Daytime Dating is divided into three parts:.................... 25

PART 1: PREPARATION 27

A System you can use today... 29
    Approaching and transitioning 29
    Attraction... 30
    Qualification.. 31
    Logistical progression 32

Inner game 33

Daytime mindsets... 33

Success expectations 39

The best places to meet women in the daytime........... 41
    The street... 41
    Shopping Malls 42
    Stores... 42
    Coffee shops.. 43
    Museums and art galleries 43
    Buses, trains and subways.. 43

The Love Systems triad 45

Introduction to the triad 45

The emotional progression model 52

The physical progression model 56

The logistical progression model 62

Putting it all together – Implications 65

Love Systems triad in daytime dating 68

PART 2: EMOTIONAL PROGRESSION 71

Chapter 5: Approaching 73

What is approaching? 73

Approaching in daytime dating 74

Verbal elements of the approach 75

Non-verbal elements of the approach 78

Approach logistics 79

Advanced considerations 81

Indirect approaches 83

How to make a direct approach work 84

Chapter summary 87

Chapter 6: Transitioning 89

Forming the Approach Habit 90

Chapter 7: Attraction 97

What is attraction? 97

Attraction in daytime dating 98

Snapshot theory 99

The attraction switches 100

Accumulating Life Experience 106

How to show your value 108

Signs of attraction 111

Chapter Summary 113

Chapter 8: Qualification 115

What is qualification? 115

Qualification in daytime dating 116

Screening 117

Compliments 120

Chapter summary 122

Chapter 9: Conversation Mapping 123

What is conversation mapping? 123

Context, work & leisure 124

Mastery topics 127

Bridging 130

Dead ends 131

Investment equilibrium 133

Chapter summary 136

Chapter 10: Comfort 139

What is comfort? 139

Comfort in daytime dating 139

Sharing and empathizing 141

Physical comfort 148

Logistical comfort 149

Signs of comfort 150

Chapter summary 151

PART 3: PHYSICAL AND LOGISTICAL PROGRESSION 153

Chapter 11: Physical Progression 155

What is physical progression? 155

Physical progression in daytime dating 155

Physical progression steps 156

Chapter summary 160

Chapter 12: Logistical Progression 161

What is logistical progression? 161

Logistical progression in daytime dating 161

Traditional dates 162

Instant dates 163

Chapter summary 165

Chapter 13: Case Studies 167

John and Sarah – John's story 167

John and Sarah – Sarah's story 168

Ravi and Anna – Ravi's story 169

Ravi and Anna – Anna's story 171

The Spanish Brunette – Jeremy Soul's story 172

Airport Pick Up – Leko's story 175

Conclusion 177

BONUS CHAPTERS 179

Introduction to Approach Anxiety 181

Chapter 14: What is Approach Anxiety? 183

How modern social programming complicates things… 183

Chapter 15: Why should you approach women? 185

It is part of your DNA – embrace it, don't fight it! 185

Take action and get your dopamine hit! 185

Nobody can reject you based on a cold approach 186

The faster you fail, the faster you succeed! 186

Have no regrets 187

You need to filter for women who meet your standards 187

It's difficult to meet women if you don't meet women 187

Realize how much power you have 188

Women love to be approached but 95% of men have no approach skill 189

Consider the 8 attraction switches 189

Chapter 16: Some Practical Tips to get Going 191

Fix your inner game! 191

Get in state 192

Be consistent – find your window! 193

Get a wingman 193

Set realistic goals 193

Sticks and carrots 194

Keep a success journal 195

The 3-second rule 195

Short-setting: 196

Conclusion 198

Chapter 17: Master Your Dating Life in One Year 201

Introduction by Joshua Farmer 201

The Pareto Principle 203

The 80/20 of dating science 204

Selective ignorance 210

Parkinson's law 212

Goal setting 213

A sample training plan for a week of night time approaching 216

Appendix 219

Glossary 221

Resources 223

- An overall system – Magic Bullets 223
- Routines – a foundation 224
- 21st century pickup – text and phone game 225
- Workshops and training 225
- Selected advanced material 227
- Advanced material, by topic 227
- Keep up to date 234
- Conclusion 235
- Testimonials 237

Room for your notes 244

Preface

How would I describe Jeremy Soul in daytime dating?
A master of speech, thought and action. Let me explain.

It was on a cold winter's day that I arrived at Stockholm international airport, primed for my first ever bootcamp as an instructor for Love Systems, the most prestigious and respected dating science company in the world. Bootcamps are intense training weekends where clients learn about every aspect of meeting, dating and approaching women – typically using bars and nightclubs to practice. I knew this was going to be life-changing weekend for me as well as our clients.

On my phone was the number of a true legend, famed for being the best daytime pick up artist in the world: "Jeremy Soul." As I walked through the terminal, I dialed the number and put the phone to my ear, not completely sure what to expect.

"Hello?"

"Hey, it's Mr M here."

"Hey mate, how are you? I'm at the airport. Can you see me?"

I scanned the area. And then I saw him. Across the hallway, stood a short, average looking guy of Sri Lankan descent, wearing jeans, a tracksuit top and professor-like glasses, with a phone to his ear, waving and looking directly at me. My first thought was, "Is this an academic or one of the world's greatest pick up artists?" Did he look like the stereotypical "geek"? Not quite. A Casanova? Definitely not at face value. Well, not until later, when I saw him work his magic.

I had heard much about Jeremy. This man was a widely revered Lothario, earmarked by respected members of the dating science community as one of the greatest seducers to climb into the international limelight.

As I approached, he smiled, put his hand out and shook my hand warmly. Over the next hour, as we shared a taxi together, we shared our thoughts about dating science, our backgrounds. What struck me was how positive and well balanced he was.

The first night we went out, I was standing next to him, with dozens of stunning Swedish girls around us in one of Stockholm's most exclusive bars. I made a comment to Jeremy about how hot the group of blondes that were standing in a tight knit group in the corner was. It looked like an impenetrable fortress and I'd watched guy after guy get shot down trying to approach them.

Jeremy smiled, and without hesitating, without blinking an eye, and with Spartan fearlessness and confidence akin to the soldiers from the movie 300, Jeremy walked towards the group. But this is where it gets amazing.

The man walked right into the middle of the group and confidently, with George Clooney-esque charm, said to the most beautiful woman, "I was standing over there with my friend, I saw you over here and thought you looked beautiful. I had to come and talk to you." It worked. The girl started beaming from ear to ear and her friends stood back, allowing Jeremy space to continue to work his charm on her.

Three minutes later, Jeremy was leaning against the bar having an intimate conversation with this beautiful woman, his hand on hers, her eyes widening and her mouth increasingly ajar with every fresh sentence he uttered. She had those puppy-dog eyes and the look on her face that said, "Who is this guy and why am I so attracted to him right now?"

Despite the fact that he had barely introduced himself to them, the other girls in the group knew that they couldn't interrupt the intensity of the moment their friend was having with this perfect stranger. All they could do was look on flabbergasted: who was this short, dark-skinned man to apparently have bigger balls than all of the other taller, better looking guys in the bar, who surely should be the ones picking up their friend?

As I spent more time with Jeremy that weekend, I saw that it wasn't just about the courage he had in moments like that. It was his ability to charm people, to excite their emotions, to make them feel appreciated and understood like no other, and to help them become stronger.

*This was a man of **action**.*

The first time I heard about Jeremy's daytime techniques, I was skeptical. I had been studying dating and pick up science for years and I thought it was impossible to get consistent results from daytime approaches, especially with a direct approach. I wasn't a believer. After spending more time with Jeremy, I became one. He made me more than that in fact – he made me a fan.

I traveled with Jeremy the world over and he showed me what was possible with daytime dating. He was meeting beautiful women on the street, in parks, cafés, shopping malls and bookstores and they would end up in bed with him at night. Every time I met one of Jeremy's girlfriends and asked him how they met, the answer was, "in the daytime." As I do with all those whom I think are great at dating science, I sat him down, asked him how he does it and listened. And listened. And listened.

This was a man of **thought**.

I count Jeremy as a work colleague and one of my closest friends. Together, we walk on a path of self-enlightenment.

This is a man whom I respect and credit with showing me what was possible in terms of meeting women in the daytime. I have not met anyone with the same sort of skill that he has in the cold light of day, unless they are people that he has trained personally.

This book is Jeremy's **speech**.

Read it. Use its ideas in your life and it will help you realize your potential with women.

Gandhi's wife was once asked by a journalist how he accomplished so much. "Simple," said the wife. "Gandhi is congruent in regards to his speech, thought and action."

And that is how Jeremy has become the leading international authority on daytime dating. Speech, thought and most importantly, action.

To my friend Jeremy Soul, I extend my heartfelt congratulations and my utmost admiration for your endeavor. I witnessed firsthand how much of a labor of love this was for you and how it represents the essence of what you have learned the hard way over the years.

Rest assured that it will touch the lives of many men and women for the better.

Mr. M

www.lovesystems.com/mr-m

Introduction

If you told me years ago I would one day write a book on how to meet and attract women, I would never have believed you.

I was a terribly introverted kid. Everything I've done in my life since about age 12 has been to try to buck that trend. When I was young, I thought that because I was short, Sri Lankan and not a good-looking kid, I could never be good with girls. Then one day I found Love Systems: I started learning about how to meet and attract women (what we call "game"), and my life began to change.

I worked hard on myself for years to get to where I am now: a full-time Love Systems instructor, traveling the world running live workshops, spending time with wonderful women and living my passions. I can't tell you how many ups and downs I've had over the years. But no matter how many times I fell off the horse, I kept getting back on it, more determined each time.

I have had more successes and failures in dating than most people I know. As the saying goes, "To succeed quickly, fail fast." So I went out there, day after day, and made all the mistakes I could. Then things began to click. Years later, I finally feel like I understand female psychology and meeting and dating beautiful and intriguing women isn't a side interest or even my job; it's just a part of my life.

Now I teach men all around the world how to meet and date beautiful women. It is incredibly rewarding to get emails from clients who are getting married, have found amazing girlfriends, or are otherwise experiencing all the fun and joy they always wanted.

Over the years, I've had the honor of speaking at conferences around the world on dating science, been the subject of a documentary by a prestigious London film school, had an anthropologist research my teachings, and been interviewed by a number of journalists in the media.

I've also been glad to have an impact on the lives of women I've met and dated or those who have read my writings. Becoming better with women has made me a stronger man and has allowed me to help others to become stronger: more confident, more determined, more aware of how the world works and how to succeed within it. No matter whether it was a one-night encounter or a deeper and longer-lasting romance, I endeavored to leave every woman I met with an experience that she could enjoy and grow from.

Like many men, I credit the early development of my current lifestyle almost entirely to the ideas presented in Magic Bullets, the gold standard of dating bibles for men. Within a few short months of learning the ideas within it, I was talking to beautiful women in bars and nightclubs everywhere, taking phone numbers, going on dates and bringing women home with me.

But as I spent more time going out specifically in the daytime to meet women, I discovered all sorts of nuances and subtleties I hadn't expected to discover. I started experimenting, testing out new theories and concepts to figure out what worked best for dating in the daytime compared with in nightclubs and bars.

I spent years honing these skills and still continue to do so now. I love meeting incredible women anywhere – in bars, clubs, through social circles and in the daytime – but many of the best I've met have been through daytime approaches.

I'm proud of what I've created because it is a simple, effective and honest method for meeting and attracting women in the daytime. Using it might lead to seemingly natural interactions with beautiful women, but there is a very scientific structure behind it – meaning that it is fully learnable, by anyone.

Good luck on your journey, friends. I hope that I can affect the course of your life and hope to hear from you in the future.

www.lovesystems.com/jeremy-soul

www.facebook.com/jeremysoul

Acknowledgements

I am forever grateful to my family, friends and lovers who have inspired and guided me. Thanks to my mother and father, without whom I would never have had the strength and resources necessary to do what I have done. Thanks to my brother and his wonderful wife for always being there and always having the strength of heart to keep us all together, and to little Jakob and Lukas who always make me smile and giggle.

Thanks to the high school crew for giving me good times in my formative years; for coming to talk to women with me when none of us knew how but we still tried. Thanks Phil, Samir, Anish, Sutha, Vinny, Dilhan, Sachin and Cheups – you boys are the best.

Thanks to the London crew: Mike, Andy, Juan, Rich, Darren and all the other guys that practiced with me way back when we were all socially awkward but had fun nonetheless. Remember miscalibrated Thursdays?

Thanks to the Love Systems crew, without whom I wouldn't have the lifestyle, abundance of pleasure, or friends I have today. Thanks Sheriff, my original mentor and the man to whom I owe so much, Savoy, Mr M, Braddock, Rokker, Kisser, Prestige, Sphinx, Cajun, Moxie, Big Business, Tenmagnet, The Don, 5.0 and Vercetti – I have learned so much from all of you.

Thanks to the Project Rockstars: Starlight, Keychain, Black Swan, Paladin, Optimist and Prizefighter. Wow, what a journey, eh?

Thanks Sebastian, Ryan, Martin, Peter, Joshua and Shak. You've all had immeasurable impact on my character and will never know how much you have helped me become the man I am today.

Thanks Nina, Amanda, Debby, Thérèse, Alev, Sonia, Marie, Katherine and Kim. You've all inspired and guided me in countless and diverse ways. Should our ways have parted or part in the future, good luck in achieving everything you could ever want.

I would also like to thank Aaron Wolverton for all the graphic design associated with this book.

This book is dedicated to Neil, who left this world far sooner than he should have and reminds me of why I choose to live each day as I do.

Magic Bullets

I direct men who have problems talking to women or want to improve their dating lives to read Magic Bullets, the gold standard of seduction bibles written by Nick Savoy, one of the world's top dating experts and President of Love Systems. It is a resource that is unparalled by any other in its depth and breadth of knowledge concerning female psychology, approaching, dating, and seducing beautiful women.

The ideas in Magic Bullets give you the foundations for a successful dating life. I can't recommend it enough to better understand female psychology and to become an attractive man. On my live workshops, clients who have read Magic Bullets or taken a bootcamp generally get more out of it than those who have never done so. But whereas Magic Bullets is a system for all forms of dating and seduction in general (including daytime, social circle, nightclubs etc.), in this book I have the freedom to focus exclusively on daytime dating.

I wrote this book for the man who from time to time sees a beautiful woman walking past him, sitting next to him on the subway or browsing a magazine in a bookstore and wonders, "How can I talk to her?" Reading this book will give you enough information to go out and meet wonderful women in almost any daytime venue, to talk with them, date them and bring them home with you.

Differences in Daytime Dating

You may be familiar with the Love Systems Triad model described by Savoy in Magic Bullets 2.0, consisting of three strands: Emotional, Physical and Logistical Progression. Further, Emotional Progression can be divided into six phases: Approaching, Transitioning, Attraction, Qualification, Comfort and Seduction.

I've conceptualized daytime interactions with women in a similar but slightly different way. The subtle nuances of dating and how to apply the Triad principles most effectively in the daytime will be explained throughout the book in great detail, but let's take an overview of some of the major differences that Magic Bullets readers will notice:

- **A specific "Inner Game" chapter for the daytime.** So many guys have problems approaching and talking to a woman when they don't have alcohol or the anonymity of a dark club environment to protect them that I included specific information to give you the right mindsets for dating in the daytime.

- **There is a greater focus on direct approaches** (whereas Magic Bullets covers direct, indirect and at least four other types of approach). I've included information on indirect approaches, but having experimented with both, I've found direct approaches to be the most effective for daytime situations and have included a lot of detail on how to make them work.

- **Passion replaces being Challenging as an Attraction switch.** There are eight Attraction switches detailed here, as in Magic Bullets, but I've removed being Challenging in order to focus on demonstrating Passion. That's not to say that being a challenge to a woman isn't important and useful, but rather that within the context of most daytime interactions, Passion is a more useful source of building attraction than trying to challenge her. In most cases, a woman is so impressed that you came to approach her in the daytime that you don't need to be as much of a challenge that you would be at night in a bar or club.

- **Qualification is covered in more detailed in terms of screening and rewarding.** The daytime is a great time to meet the kind of women you really want to, so I've included a lot of detail on setting your standards and screening women to meet them. There's also a lot of focus on the right way to appreciate women – compliments can be used far more often and more powerfully in the daytime than at night.

- **Comfort is analyzed and described in a greater level of detail.** Whereas nighttime interactions typically involve a lot of Attraction and Qualification time, Comfort is going to be more significant with women you meet in the daytime. So I've described the relevant factors for Comfort here and shown you how to apply it when talking to a woman in a café, bookstore etc. (or that can applied later when you are on a date with her).

- **Seduction (what to do when a woman is in your bedroom) is not covered in** this book, because whether you meet a woman in the nighttime or the daytime, it's pretty much the same process. Refer to Magic Bullets for information on that.

- **Physical Progression is focused on less in the early stages of the interaction.** In a nightclub or bar, a higher level of touching is expected and accepted, but in the daytime you will generally have to focus more on your conversational ability. Of course, you still need to progress things physically and logistically, so I have covered these two Triad strands in the final part of the book.

Caveats

I want to stress that the information presented here comes with a few caveats. Some people make the mistake of taking things 100% literally and believe that if it's written by someone who is a guru, then it must be gospel.

At Love Systems, the barriers to entry for becoming an instructor are indeed high. I had to prove myself in-field and on bootcamps for a long time before Savoy gave me the green light to start teaching programs. But just because we are all good at what we do and teach, it doesn't mean that we know everything there is to know about dating. One of the things we pride ourselves on is continuing to learn and evolve as a community and as men who are good with women.

So understand that as I write this book, I believe it to be the most up-to-date, effective and powerful system for meeting women in the daytime. But bear the following caveats in mind:

1. **The sequence of the Love Systems Triad described here is a model.** The fact is that there will always be situations where things happen out of sequence. Interactions won't always progress in exactly this order, but they will tend to.

2. **Don't get hung up on terminology.** For ease of learning and for the benefit of the tens of thousands of people who've read Magic Bullets or are on The Attraction Forums (the Love Systems online community), I've tried to use terminology that's consistent with how people talk about dating and attraction today. Whether you call it "rapport" or "comfort," or "day game" or "daytime dating" isn't as important as what you actually do and say when you are with women.

3. **You will only truly understand this information when you put it into practice.** It's great to read Daytime Dating, but you won't fully believe in what I advise here until you try it for yourself. Go out and use this stuff.

How to use this book

This book has been written to be both a companion to Magic Bullets for those wishing to understand more about daytime dating and as a stand-alone book for those who are new to the idea of actively working to improve their interactions with women.

If at the end of this book, you feel like you need further information on a specific topic (for example, meeting women through your social circle or relationship management), then I've included a bunch of Resources at the end that will help you.

In particular, there is information in the Resources section on the live Daytime Dating workshops that we run and how you might benefit from them. The workshops involve not only training of the theoretical material, but live coaching "in-field" by expert instructors. Our training is second-to-none, and if you find yourself needing further assistance to apply the material presented here, I highly recommend looking into it – you'll find it nothing less than life-changing.

Daytime Dating is divided into three parts:

- **Preparation.** This section will help to prepare you mentally for the challenges you'll face. Most men get incredibly nervous when approaching women in the daytime (I was no different when I started). This section will help you to deal with that, set healthy expectations for yourself and introduce you to the foundational model of everything we do at Love Systems, the Love Systems Triad.

- **Emotional Progression.** This section focuses on progressing things emotionally as you talk to a woman, including how to approach her and begin a conversation (Approaching and Transitioning), how to get her interested in you (Attraction), how to show your interest in her (Qualification), how to structure the initial conversation

(Conversation Mapping) and how to build an emotional connection with her (Comfort).

- **Physical and Logical Progression.** This section will show you how to progress the interaction to the point where she is in your bedroom and things get physical between the two of you.

DAYTIME DATING: Never Sleep Alone

PART I
PREPARATION

A System you can use today

Being able to successfully approach and date women in the daytime is a skill that takes time to learn. As you practice with the information you learn in this book, gradually things will begin to "click" and you will find your interactions with attractive women becoming better.

There is a lot of information presented here and it will take you time to read. A lot of things will make more sense once you go out and try it a few times and observe the results. So treat this book as a reference that you keep coming back to, over and over again.

However, you might be sitting in a café reading this right now and there is a cute girl sitting next to you. Or you might walk out of your office at lunchtime and see a beautiful woman walking past you on the street. So what should you say?

Well, this entire book is devoted to breaking down the stages you need to go through to successfully approach and date women in these situations. However, this section will show you very briefly how to get into that initial conversation and take it somewhere, for example taking a phone number.

This is by no means a comprehensive explanation of daytime dating, but should be enough if you only have ten minutes to read this and a beautiful woman happens to cross your path today.

Approaching and transitioning

Get her attention politely, explain how you came to notice her and pay her a small, but genuine physical compliment. For example:

- *Excuse me, hi. I just saw you sitting there and I had to tell you, you have an amazing style. I really love your look: it's so well put-together.*

- *Excuse me, hi. I just saw you sitting there and I had to tell you, you have an amazing style. I really love your look, it's so well put-together.*

- Wait for her to say thank you, then put your hand out, ask her name and introduce yourself.

- The ideal reaction from a woman is pleasant surprise. The more warmly she reacts, the more open to a conversation she is. If you get a less than warm re action, don't take it personally! Some women just aren't interested in meeting strangers, or perhaps she already has a boyfriend.

- The and chapters cover all this in a lot of detail, showing you ways to make it work as effectively as possible.

Attraction

- Over the next five or ten minutes, you want to find out a little bit about who this woman is, and demonstrate that you are an interesting person to her.

- Find out what she is doing today, what she does for a living, and what she does in her spare time for fun. Don't ask all these questions in a row, but gradually find out these answers over the course of a five- or ten-minute conversation. Use her answers to make statements that lead the conversation onto topics you are knowledgeable about.

- For example, if you're a good writer, and it turns out she's studying journalism, you could talk about how much you enjoy journalism, your experiences of studying writing, or what you love most about writing as a job.

- Make sure you don't go into interview mode by asking lots of questions and making few statements. You should make statements about yourself for most of the conversation. The questions you ask her simply allow you to target the statements you're going to make.

- Try to discover things that you are both passionate about and spend time talking about those things with her.

Qualification

- This is where you find out whether she has the kind of personality and lifestyle of someone you could get along with – someone worth getting to know better.

- Think about your favorite topics of conversation, whether it's travelling, writing, dancing, sports, music, movies or anything else, and ask her questions related to these things, for example, "What kind of movies do you like?"

- If after a few minutes, you get the impression you could genuinely like her, give her another compliment that this time doesn't relate to how she looks. For example, "I really like that you're into travelling. It makes me think that we could have a few things in common."

- Try to pay her a couple of these non-physical compliments over the course of the conversation.

Logistical progression

- If you've had a good conversation with her after five or ten minutes, tell her that you enjoyed talking with her and that you'd like to talk some more over a drink or a coffee. See how she responds.

- If she agrees, find out what her schedule is like for tonight or the next few days, and arrange a mutually convenient time to meet. Ask her to put her phone number in your phone and save it.

- You have hopefully now set up a date!

- If she says no, tell her, "No problem. It was nice to meet you," and go approach some more women...

Inner game

Approaching women in the daytime can be a scary thing to do. If you've never been particularly confident talking to women, then approaching them at night is scary enough – but at least then you have alcohol, your buddies, social proof (if you are with other women) and the anonymity of a dark, loud environment to protect your ego from rejection.

A big hurdle to jump over is making your first daytime approach. The first time I traveled into central London all those years ago to do my first "mission", which was simply walking up to ten women and telling them, "You're cute," I was terrified.

What made me overcome that? Honestly, there was nothing that special that I heard, saw or understood that gave me the confidence to do it; it was simply good old-fashioned determination. There comes a point in your life when you realize that if you want to grow, if you want to improve your life and if you want to acquire new skills or experiences, you are going to feel scared when you do so. Accept that and move beyond it, or that feeling with haunt you forever. Courage isn't the absence of fear. It's the willingness to act in spite of it.

Daytime mindsets

It's very important to have a positive and healthy mindset when it comes to approaching women in the daytime. You can do hundreds or thousands of approaches and have successes with those, but ultimately if your head is not in the right space, you are walking down a path of frustration and disappointment.

When I first started daytime approaches I didn't have all of these mindsets. But as I started to reach plateaus in my skill set and wanted more consistency in my results (and less frustration), I realized that there were several principles I needed to embrace in order to be as successful as possible. These took me years to figure out. Some of them will resonate with you immediately, whereas others will take some time to take root in your subconscious and your behavior. Keep on coming back to these mindsets whenever you feel frustrated and they will offer you solace and a route back onto the right path.

Anything is possible

When I first started daytime approaching, I thought it was impossible to talk to a woman in the cold light of day, let alone take her phone number or even take her on a date instantly. I've since blown that reality apart and taken things much further than that.

I've approached women while they were with their mothers, when they seemed like they were in a rush and wouldn't stop for me, when they were surrounded by groups of friends, and in even stranger, more awkward or difficult situations than those.

I still haven't done everything I could want to do in terms of daytime approaching, but I realize now that nothing is impossible. Some things are improbable in certain situations, but with time and energy anything is achievable.

I take risks for the things I want

I take a lot of inspiration from the lives of successful people. A few years ago I read Losing My Virginity by Richard Branson, a billionaire and the man behind the Virgin brand.

In it, Branson describes his early business endeavors such as starting a student magazine at age 16 and calling national advertisers to convince them to advertise in his unheard-of publication. He goes on to describe how someone offered him a stake in a new airline. Against all personal and business advice from those around him, he took up the challenge: the now successful airline Virgin Atlantic was born.

As I read Branson's book, I realized that there was one major quality that set him apart from most of the world: he is willing to take risks for the things he wants. He says,

> *"My interest in life comes from setting myself huge, apparently unachievable challenges and trying to rise above them...from the perspective of wanting to live life to the fullest, I felt that I had to attempt it."*

Taking risks is not about always achieving what you want. There will be failures and things that don't work out; you need to accept that. Taking risks is about being willing to act when you think, "I want that." The outcome is not as important as taking action.

When I go to bed at night, I don't think of how many women I've slept with or how deep I've fallen in love. I think about how much opportunity I've seen and how much of that I've acted on. Living a life with beautiful, intelligent and inspirational women around you is great, but what is really satisfying is living a life of action instead of one of regret. The way you choose to live your life is infinitely more important than the external trappings of your life; success in the latter is great, but it doesn't come without the former.

Every time you see a woman in the daytime you want to talk to, remember that the uncomfortable feeling of approaching her and potentially getting rejected will subside a lot quicker and be a lot more bearable than the regret you will feel if you don't. Be happy to take the risk for something you want, and don't worry so much about the outcome of each individual situation.

I express my desires and feelings

Doing daytime approaches is like putting a microscope on your social interactions. Suddenly, everything appears to you in a level of detail and intensity that you have never experienced before; not in nightclub approaches, social circle introductions, or even in speed dating.

You have a few seconds as a beautiful woman walks past you to decide whether you are going to run after her and say something, anything, or let her be just another missed opportunity. In nightclubs and bars, you can often get away with a little procrastination. In the daytime, rarely do you have that luxury. The window of opportunity opens and closes in moments.

If you are a person that rationalizes, calculates and takes time to figure out the best strategy for the highest chance of success with her, you could miss out on more opportunities in the daytime than those you capitalize on.

I'm not saying there is no place for strategy or planning in the daytime, but you need to be willing to act quickly lest all your strategizing be wasted.

The simplest way to do this is to be willing to express your desires and feelings as soon as you feel them. You see a woman you like, you notice something about her, and then you approach her and tell her immediately. The more time you spend thinking about it and rationalizing what could happen, the greater the chance you will get nervous and miss the opportunity.

Expressing how you feel by telling a woman that you love the way she carries herself or the way her hair bounces off her shoulders gives you satisfaction in an instant and makes you a stronger man. Most men are afraid to express how they feel; embracing your desires like this sets you apart as a higher caliber man.

The counterpart of this mindset is that you are happy to simply express your desires without expectation or outcome. It is more about putting yourself out there and giving her the opportunity to spend time with you than it is about expecting or hoping that she will feel similarly.

For example, the worst way you can tell a woman you love her is to say it expecting her to say it back. Do that and you are a weak man. Tell a woman you love her without worry whether she will say it back or not and you are a strong man. I once called a woman to tell her I loved her. Three months later she called me to say that she realized she felt the same way. Was I worried in between? No. I was happy to simply express how I felt and to continue spending time with her.

It's the same with daytime approaches. Be happy to simply express your desires and feelings when you first approach her. If you spend more time with her, go on a date, or end up in bed a few hours later, great. But live a life where you embrace and express your desires instead of hiding them inside and you will lead a much happier life.

I am coming from a position of high value

It's very easy when you're talking to or looking at a beautiful woman to think she is "out of your league," that she somehow has more value than you. As soon as you start to think that, it's intimidating.

But what happens when you start talking to her? Maybe it turns out she is a student of an academic subject that you have a PhD in. Maybe she goes regularly to a nightclub where you know the manager. Maybe when you wake up with her in the morning, you will realize that she is a person just like you, with strengths and weaknesses of her own, and insecurities deeper than you could possibly imagine.

Value is relative across situations. Sure, when you're in a nightclub and she is dancing on the pole, she has every guy in there gawping at her. She might have higher social value than you in that situation (because more people are focusing on her than they are on you). But take her out of that environment and put her in your workplace as your intern or junior. Suddenly you have the higher value.

That's just one example, yet there are countless situations where you might hold greater value than her. You will never have higher value than every person you meet in life, but if you recognize the areas of your life where you do have strong value, then you have something to offer everyone.

When you are talking to a woman in the daytime, realize that you are coming from a position of high value. You will convey some of this value immediately as you approach her (your body language, tonality etc.), but the rest of it will be conveyed as you talk more to her. Don't worry about demonstrating it all straight away. Relax, do enough to get her interested in the approach, and believe that she will like you more as you interact with her.

You see her walking down the street, she's beautiful, sure. But aren't you yourself intelligent, funny, and interesting? It might not be immediately apparent when she looks at you, but take the chance to talk to her and she might just discover all these things about you (especially with what you are going to learn in this book).

I want you, but I do not need you

There's a big paradox here which astute readers may have noticed. If you adopt all the above mindsets – you realize you are high value, you just enjoy expressing how you feel – then what is the point or rationale behind seeking outcome (sex, love or otherwise) at all?

Is it wrong to want to enjoy the physicality of a beautiful woman, or to relish the companionship an intelligent woman offers? No.

What is dangerous is to think that you need any of this in the absolute sense. In absolute terms, all you need is food, air and water.

Realize that you have romantic and sexual desires and be willing to act on them (as described above). These desires are real and are a part of you, but they do not control you. Each woman you meet might be desirable (she might even be the most desirable woman you have ever met in your life), but she is not necessary for your existence or happiness.

This is the most powerful mindset you can ever adopt for your dating life and indeed other areas of your life. Buddhists believe that detachment from outcome and the external trappings of life is important for spiritual self-satisfaction. But if that was true, why not cast off your clothes, give away all your money, and go live on a mountain somewhere by yourself?

It's good to have desires and to want things. It makes for an interesting life to pursue these desires and achieve your goals (and to keep on setting and achieving new goals). But it's bad to think that any one outcome is the be all and end all of your life.

Some time ago I got into a stupid fight and ended up in hospital with my left eye pretty damaged. I wasn't sure whether I'd ever be able to see out of it again. As I lay there in the hospital the next morning, I thought to myself, "Whatever happens, I will deal with it." I was amazed at my own stoicism, and I realized it has come from the path I have been walking for the last few years in dating science.

There is an immense inner strength you develop when you become a person who is willing to try to achieve everything he wants in life, and willing to deal with any outcome as a result of those efforts. Positive or negative, whatever happens to you in your life makes for a more interesting tapestry overall.

So every time you want to talk to a beautiful woman you see walking past you, embrace your desire for her but realize that whatever happens, you are still you, and that is all you need.

Success expectations

You won't become a master of daytime dating overnight. It's impossible to say how long it will take you before you reach a particular benchmark of being "good" because everyone starts from a different place (based on their genetics, early upbringing, formative experiences at school and the influences they've had since then) and learns at a different rate. Being "good" is also relative; knowing that you are implementing what you are learning and making improvements is a more useful measure of success.

You will have to take yourself out of your comfort zone regularly by doing things that are deeply unfamiliar or unusual for you. It may seem strange to start having conversations with women using the structure and techniques you are going to learn. You will have to feign confidence and pretend you know what you are doing for a while: at least until you have practiced the elements so much that they become natural to you and you no longer have to think about them.

You may be using pre-scripted lines and stories (what are called "routines") in order to gain confidence and competence in having interesting conversations with women. Don't worry if it feels artificial at first – it will. When you feel ready to free-flow attractive conversation, try not using anything scripted and see how you do.

The important thing is that you are progressing and growing in your ability to meet and attract women. If you find that your progress slows and then stops, you probably need additional information to guide you to the next stage of your development. The Resources chapter at the end of this book should provide you with enough direction on where to go next.

Don't set goals like, "I want to be able to seduce every woman I see." When you encounter a group of guys socially, at a business conference or at school, you don't think to yourself, "I am going to make friends with all of these guys here," do you?

No, you don't. Because you know that some of them you will like and get along with, while others you won't really have anything in common with or want to get to know better. Why should it be any different with women?

Yes it's true that we prioritize physical beauty more so than women, but other factors still come into play when we think about bringing a woman into our lives. Believe me, sex with a woman who is beautiful inside and out, whom you still want to be there when you wake up in the morning, is a much longer-lasting and fulfilling source of pleasure than someone whom you are tolerating until you can orgasm and roll over.

My goal is to teach you how to bring quality women into your life through the power of daytime dating. If you find yourself happily dating a wonderful woman, or being able to have romantic and sexual encounters with beautiful, intelligent and interesting women wherever you are, then I'll be very proud of what I've brought to your attention in this book.

The best places to meet women in the daytime

The beauty of daytime dating is that the world is your playground. You don't have to try to get into an exclusive club late on a Saturday night, talk over loud music or call a bunch of your friends to try to convince them to come party with you.

Daytime dating is also a flexible form of meeting women. You can talk to women on your way to and from work, on lunch breaks, while you're running errands, while you're working on your laptop in a café or when you're grocery shopping. There are countless possibilities.

In addition to flexibility, it also offers a diversity of women. Nightclubs and bars tend to be full of women who like going out, drinking or partying, which can of course be fun. But what if you want to meet women who love to read, go to art galleries, or sit in cafés chatting and drinking coffee with friends?

Any venue where you might possibly find attractive women is fair game. Let's look at some examples.

The street

This is my favorite venue because you get constant streams of beautiful women walking past, provided you pick the right street of course. Shopping streets are ideal, but beware of times when they're overcrowded. Women are more "on edge" when there are a lot of people bustling by them, so it's a good idea in these cases to wait until there is some space around her when she can reasonably stop before you approach.

Also, be aware that people are constantly going in and out of stores, crossing roads etc., so when you see a woman you want to approach you should do so quickly or she could change her trajectory suddenly and it might look as though you're stalking her. You can get away with a little hesitation in bars and clubs (though it's not ideal and you should try to eliminate it) because the women aren't going anywhere, but on the street you really do need to act quickly.

Shopping Malls

These are always full of good-looking women, either hanging out by themselves, or more commonly in groups. During the week you'll tend to find a lot of women who are tourists, bored or just not in nine-to-five jobs. These women tend to be interested in adventure, so approaching them makes for some great interactions!

On the weekends you'll tend to find more party girls out shopping or getting ready for their nights out. These women can be just as fun, and you can usually arrange some interesting meet-ups in the evening if you find out what their plans are that night.

Be careful of spending too long in shopping malls and doing too many approaches while you're there. If you roam the mall and do dozens of approaches in a short space of time, people might notice and it could get socially awkward.

Stores

There's a huge variety of stores that you can have a lot of fun with. Bookstores and music stores are great because you can meet women that have similar tastes to you and start conversations related to these.

The caveat I'd add to approaching women in stores is to be very aware of your surroundings. Certain stores are less conducive to approaching (for example, you'd have to work hard to establish credibility for why you're in a women's lingerie store). Be aware also that store security might see you talking to their customers and won't appreciate you hitting on all of them! So be discreet and don't chase every woman you see around the store.

Coffee shops

You won't always find huge volumes of beautiful women in a café the same way you might a bar or a club, but you will spot the occasional woman or group of women you want to approach. Coffee shops also have the unique characteristic that people are usually sitting down instead of being on the move and therefore often have more time for a conversation and/or adventure.

Coffee shops are also great when you have a laptop to work from or a book to read. If you were going to work from home or just sit around and read your book, why not do so in a coffee shop where a stream of beautiful women will be passing through as you sit?

I often approach women in coffee shops either when I am leaving, or they are on their way out. That way, if it doesn't go well, you don't have to continue sitting near them and feeling awkward. If it does go well, you can talk with them for a few minutes before you or they move on.

Museums and art galleries

These venues don't necessarily have a high flow of beautiful women passing through, but suit men who are looking for older, more creative-minded women. Again, as with book and music stores, it's easy to strike up conversations and find people with similar tastes to you.

Buses, trains and subways

Depending on what city you live in, public transport approaches can be an amazing way to maximize your time and opportunity for women. Be strategic. In some cities (for example, London, New York, Toronto, San Francisco) it is normal for beautiful women to be on the subway or a bus. In others (for example, Los Angeles, Philadelphia or San Diego), a little less so.

One thing you will notice after approaching a few women on public transport is a real time constraint. You might only have a few stops on the subway before she gets off, so it's important to find out early on in the interaction where she is headed so you know what timeframe to work to so you can get her contact details in time.

The Love Systems triad

The foundation of the daytime dating system is the Love Systems Triad, originally conceived by Nick Savoy. As he's the expert on it, I'm going to pass over to him for this chapter to give an overview of the Triad model and how it applies to daytime dating (and I'll go over each part of the model in greater detail in the chapters to come).

The Love Systems Triad is a powerful system to develop sexual or romantic relationships with beautiful women, even if you're not rich, famous, or good-looking yourself.

It is based on real-world experience from hundreds of thousands of "approaches" and "pickups" - both through "cold approach" (approaching women you don't know) and "social circle" (friends, co-workers, etc.).

Have I approached hundreds of thousands of women? Of course not. But I do have the good fortune of having a team of over twenty Love Systems instructors worldwide, and a broader network of thousands of clients who we've taught in person. By constantly testing and refining ideas, we've evolved a system that works regardless of a man's age, culture, or background. It's based on what actually works in the real world – it has to be, because it's what we use ourselves.

Introduction to the triad

Most women – especially beautiful women who are used to a lot of attention from men - won't sleep with someone new unless at least three specific factors are present:

- She feels the right kind of emotional connection with you.
- She has a physical connection with you.
- The two of you are alone somewhere where sex can reasonably happen (Logistics).

Now, it's not quite as easy as flipping a switch (or three switches). There is usually a bunch of intermediate steps on the way to her being emotionally, physically, and logistically ready to sleep with you. It's like driving a car. You don't usually go straight into fifth gear; you build momentum by accelerating through the gears in the right order until you're going full speed.

I'll give you a quick idea of how this all works, using the "the right kind of emotional connection" as an example.

INSIGHT #1: THE FOUR KEY EMOTIONS

One thing we learned from our hundreds of thousands of approaches is that women around the world generally want to feel four specific emotions before they say yes:

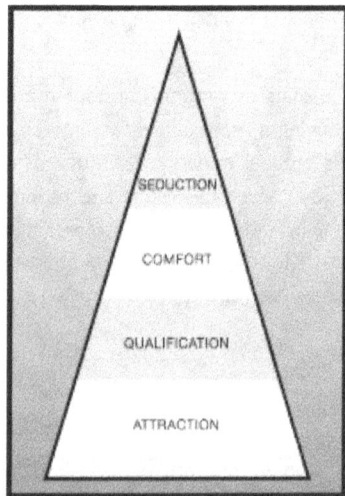

1. Feeling that your social value is equal to or greater than hers (Attraction).

2. Feeling that she's earned your attention for non-superficial reasons (Qualification).

3. Feeling comfort and connection with you (Comfort).

4. Being aroused by you without awkwardness or embarrassment (Seduction).

INSIGHT #2: THE MAGIC SEQUENCE

This one amazed us at first. Not only did we discover the four key emotions, but we learned that they're most effective when a woman feels them in exactly that order.

Therefore, we call this sequence of emotions the Emotional Progression Model, and each emotion is a "phase" in the Model.

Why does the order matter? Let's use my friend Tim as an example. Like many men who haven't studied Love Systems, when Tim meets a woman he is interested in, he starts asking her a lot of questions without adding anything interesting to the conversation. Have you ever had a conversation like this?

> Tim: Hi, I'm Tim.
>
> Jennifer: I'm Jennifer.
>
> Tim: Where are you from?
>
> Jennifer: New York.
>
> Tim: Oh cool. What are you doing here?
>
> Jennifer: Just visiting some friends.
>
> Tim: Oh cool. So what do you do?
>
> Jennifer: I'm a nurse. Listen, it's been nice talking to you, but I have to get going.

Why did Tim fail? The simple answer is he wasn't man enough to ask for help. Men ask each other for help on their taxes, golf swings, and cars, but most guys get all stubborn when it comes to getting help on something much more important – your romantic and sex life.

Fortunately, as a reader of this book, you won't have this problem. You will be able to surpass Tim and all of the other "Tims" of the world. Congratulations - you've already gotten past the biggest hurdle to lifelong success with beautiful women.

Tim's second mistake was that he got the emotional steps in the wrong order. He started off by asking Jennifer to share details of her life. In other words, he tried to build Comfort.

Unfortunately, beautiful women tend to get approached all the time by men asking lots of these sorts of Comfort-questions without showing any social value themselves. Jennifer has probably learned that these conversations usually end with some nervous guy asking her out, and an awkward situation when she's not interested. So she shut Joe down before the conversation could get there.

The problem is that Tim hasn't yet shown her that he is worth her time. Asking a woman about herself isn't wrong; it was just a bad idea to ask so many questions before he gave her a few reasons to invest in the conversation (which happens in the Attraction phase). If Tim were very good looking, that might have given her a reason, or if she had been feeling lonely or insecure, or whatever. But that's not what Love Systems is about. I want you to be able to succeed with secure and confident beautiful women, regardless of your looks.

Let the sequence be a guide, not a straightjacket. Think of it like you have three glasses, and you need to fill them all with water. These glasses represent your Attraction, Qualification, and Comfort levels with a specific woman. Fill them in that order, but remember that water, like emotions, can evaporate. A woman who felt attracted to you last week (or even an hour ago, at a busy and exciting shopping mall) might not feel as attracted to you right now. This can happen during the same conversation if you let her Attraction levels dissipate once you've moved on to Qualification and Comfort. In these situations, you have to 'top up' the Attraction glass while in a later phase.

Incidentally, this is why first phone calls and first dates should usually begin with "refreshing" her Attraction, Qualification, and Comfort levels before you break new ground.

In case you are wondering, you can't prepare for this "evaporation" by giving a woman "extra" Attraction, Qualification, or Comfort early on. In other words, you can't overfill a glass to save some for later. This is a common mistake when men first learn Love Systems Attraction techniques, and figure that more is better. It's not. Trying to attract a woman who is already attracted won't make her more into you; it's more likely to frustrate her and cause her to lose interest altogether.

INSIGHT #3: FAST TRACK TO MASTERY

Our discovery that the phases of the Emotional Progression Model should be accomplished in a specific order had a surprising benefit, beyond bringing our ability to succeed with beautiful women to the next level. It made Love Systems much easier to learn and use, because it maps directly to how most men actually think and break down problems. It was almost like nature (or Cupid) had meant for us to discover this all along...

Unlike women, men are not natural multi-taskers. The male brain is best at accomplishing a series of logically connected steps, one a time, toward a goal. The Emotional Progression Model not only allows for this, it insists on it.

For example, once you're in a conversation with a woman, your main goal is to make her feel attracted to you. Once that's done, all you have to think about – emotionally – is making her feel that she's earned your attention for non-superficial reasons (i.e., Qualification). And so on. (Yes, I know that "build Attraction/Qualification/Comfort with a beautiful woman" is easier said than done, but we have the rest of the book to show you some of our techniques. Right now we're just introducing you to the overall system so you know what fits where.)

The step-by-step system also makes it easy to learn from your mistakes. You attracted her, but you lost her interest a little while later? Probably a problem with Qualification. Passed through Attraction, Qualification, and Comfort just fine but she said: "let's just be friends?" Probably a Seduction issue.

Now, it's not always as easy as "one thing at a time." You have to be thinking of all three dimensions: Emotional, Physical, and Logistical. This is one of the things that makes the Love Systems Triad so effective (and original), but it does take a bit of practice. Fortunately, all three dimensions of the Triad work in similar ways. And since there is an incredible depth of Love Systems resources for each phase of each dimension, it's easy to get expert help on any phase you want to improve.

Jeremy Soul

THE LOVE SYSTEMS TRIAD

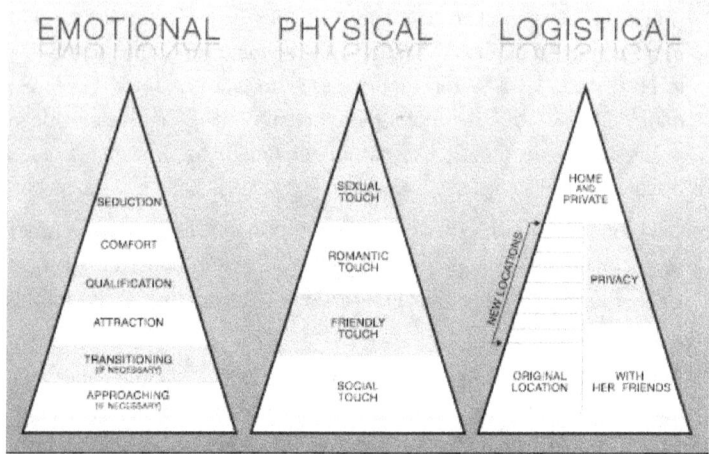

How to use the triad

In a moment, we're going to get into all of the details of all three models. But don't just plow into this if you're new. The Love Systems Triad is an amazingly sophisticated tool, but it's important to walk before you try to run.

NEW

If you're new to the Love Systems Triad...

Start with the Emotional Progression Model only. Don't worry about anything else until you are able to get to at least the Comfort phase consistently. Don't distract yourself with other information that is not part of this goal. Trust me on this one – we've trained over ten thousand men and know what works. Let Confucius inspire you: "A journey of a thousand miles begins with a single step."

INTERMEDIATE SKILLS

Use the Emotional Progression Model as your base, but keep in mind that you need to escalate physically and logistically as well. Without worrying about the specifics of the Physical or Logistical Progression Models, look for (and create) opportunities to do the following:

Initiate and intensify touching (aka "kino") between you and her. Start small and build momentum. Get her alone. A lot of times for daytime dating, this will require a phone number and a date another time. Move her. Almost any move is good, but the best moves are the ones that lead toward a bedroom.

ADVANCED SKILLS

Unlock the full power of the Love Systems Triad, using all three models and being conscious of and looking for inter-relationships between them. Read on.

The emotional progression model

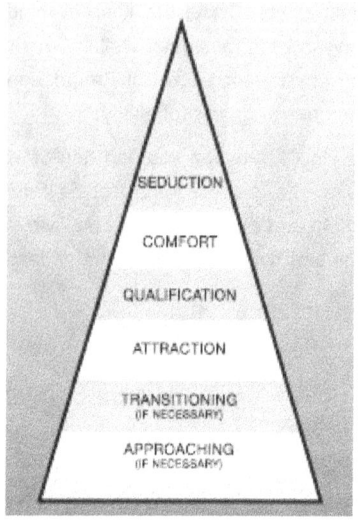

Let's explore the Emotional Progression Model in a bit more detail. Note that the point of this section is to get you up to speed so you can make the most of the material in this book. The detailed guide to the Love Systems Triad and how to use it to its full potential is the focus of a large part of our cornerstone book, Magic Bullets.

The Four Key Emotions

1. **Attraction** - *Feeling that a man's social value is equal to or greater than hers*

Every woman will perceive a man's social value differently. However, our research has shown that most women around the world respond to some of the same things. We call these "Attraction Switches." For daytime dating, these are: appearance, confidence, social intelligence, humor, passion, pre-selection, status and wealth.

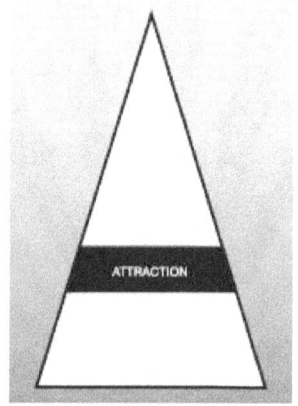

A woman's social value is based on how desirable she feels that she is at that moment to men in general. To grossly oversimplify, many beautiful women like to sleep with men who are "better" than them. This causes a woman to feel attracted to you. We call the time when you're doing this the Attraction phase (or just "Attraction").

2. **Qualification** - *Feeling that she's earned his attention for non-superficial reasons [Qualification]*

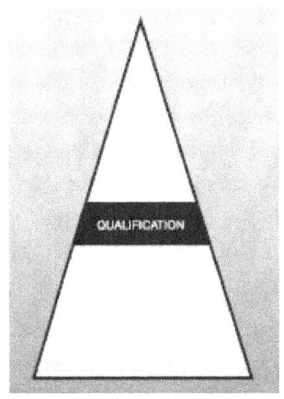

Most women like to feel that they have earned a man's attention and that he is interested in them for more than their looks. This is for two reasons. First, they know that high-value men can easily attract beautiful women. If being beautiful is enough by itself to get you interested, then she'll question whether you're really a high-value man (or she'll think you're a "player"). Second, people value what they have to work for.

The Qualification phase is where we solve both problems by 1) helping her work for your interest and then 2) giving it to her based on something other than her looks alone. The Qualification phase is usually where you make your interest more specific to her personality.

3. **Comfort** - *Feeling comfort and connection with him*

Comfort is usually the longest phase in the Emotional Progression Model. It begins toward the end of the Qualification phase, when it's clear that both of you are interested in each other. It ends when you have established enough comfort and connection with her that she is comfortable being in a sexual situation with you. A sexual situation is one in which a woman is emotionally ready to engage in sexual behavior

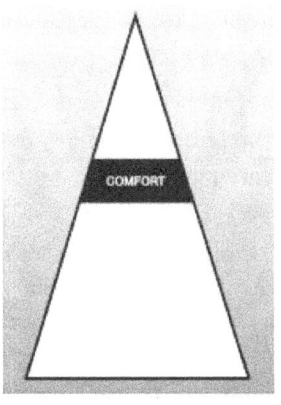

(touching that goes beyond kissing) in a place where sex could realistically happen.

4. **Seduction** - *Feeling aroused by him without awkwardness or embarrassment*

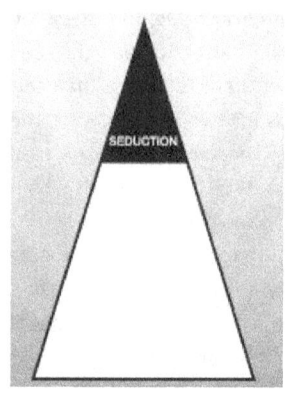

Seduction is based primarily on intensifying her willingness to have sex with you and mitigating her reasons not to. We separate the emotional process of seduction from the physical progress – the latter is called "Sexual Touch" and is part of the Physical Progression Model. We do this because the processes themselves are different.

Physically, you are trying to arouse her. Emotionally, you are trying to make her comfortable with being aroused by you.

These four emotions apply in virtually every situation – from a woman you meet on the street to a blind date with your sister's best friend.

However, if you're meeting women through "cold approach" – i.e., you don't have any reason to know each other, but you approached her on the street or in a coffee shop or wherever – then there are two phases that have to take place before she'd even be ready to be attracted to you. These are:

1. **Approaching:** *Starting a single-subject conversation*

The Approaching phase starts when you first see a woman you're interested in meeting. It ends when you start a conversation with her - usually about a specific subject. We sometimes call the different ways of starting a conversation "openers" or "opening lines."

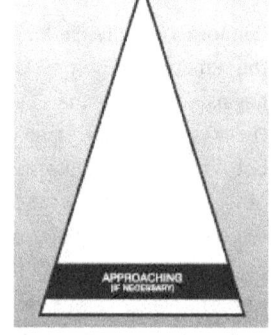

2. **Transitioing:** *Turning a single-subject approach into a normal, free-flowing conversation*

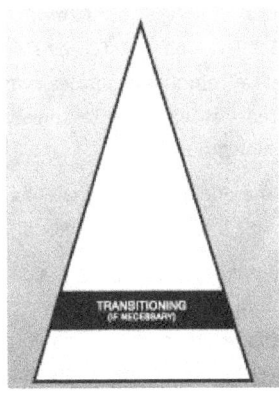

To attract a woman, you should be in a conversation with her that can include a variety of topics and where you can express emotion. We call this "normal conversation." Since it's not always easy to go straight from an opener into normal conversation, we often use a Transition. The Transition refocuses the dynamic of your interaction and shows a woman that you're about to start a multi-topic conversation with her. This can be as simple as introducing yourself or as detailed as using a specific "cold read" to get into a specific topic of conversation.

Key Tips to Remember:

1. **Attraction comes before Qualification.**
   Make a woman attracted to you before showing significant non-superficial interest in her.

2. **Attraction comes before Comfort.**
   Make a woman attracted to you before asking her for lots of personal information.

3. **Qualification comes before Comfort.**
   Have a woman work to win your interest before you open up to each other.

4. **Comfort comes before Seduction.**

Help a woman feel connected to you before progressing sexually.

The physical progression model

Earlier versions of Love Systems featured only the breakthrough concepts of the Emotional Progression Model. The idea of a step-by-step model and a correct identification of the key emotional phases was revolutionary at the time, and one of the reasons why Love Systems is recognized today as the leading dating coaching group.

Still, like any simplification, it has its limits. And one of those is that – as I often explain at our live workshops – "you can't talk a woman into bed."

To be consistently successful with beautiful women, you should master the art of the "physical conversation." This ranges from subtle signals - like when one of you reaches out to touch the other to respond to a humorous comment or to emphasize a point – to the more obvious physical advances like putting your arm around her, putting her in your lap, kissing her, or more. We call it a "conversation" because her reactions to your moves, and your reactions to hers, are equally important and build on each other in sequence.

I remember a date I was on few years ago, before I discovered Love Systems. My friend set me up. She was a graduate student, intelligent, playful, and very attractive. We had a ton in common, from taste in books and music to a shared interest in history, astronomy and classic cult movies.

I thought our date went well, with lots of laughs and great conversation. But when I tried to kiss her at the end of the night, she pulled away. Now, women will rarely tell you why they reject you, because they don't want to feel

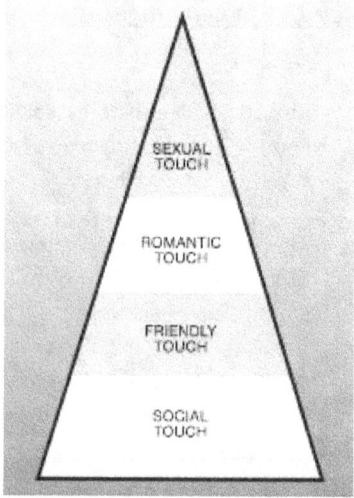

mean or have awkward conversations, but in this case I happened to run into her a couple of years later, when I was deep into developing Love Systems. I asked her if she remembered our date – she did – and she told me that she'd been really interested in me at first, but toward the end of the night the "energy" was gone and she thought of me more as a friend. Okay….but what did that actually mean?

In Love Systems terms, the lack of physical contact and physical progression over the course of the night slowly but surely dissipated her romantic/sexual feelings for me. She didn't even realize this was happening – women often don't know why they become attracted or un-attracted and their explanations are often just guesses or rationalizations of their behavior. But in this case her meaning was easy to interpret:

Emotional Progression without Physical Progression = Let's Just Be Friends

In more technical language, I'd tried to jump to the end of Romantic Touch when I hadn't even established Social Touch (we'll cover each of the phases of the Physical Progression Model in a moment). I hadn't built any momentum, and my sequencing error was the physical equivalent of Tim approaching a beautiful woman with Comfort before Attraction.

Before we dive into this, it's important to realize that "Physical Progression" isn't groping or forcing yourself on women. Rather, you are copying the intuitive touching that many charismatic men do naturally.

For example, U.S. President Bill Clinton had an amazing ability to connect with people.

The other day I was watching an old newscast, and saw him shaking hands with someone. I must have replayed it four times - there was so much going on. He shook hands with his right hand, and his left went to the other guy's elbow. Then he said a couple of words, laughed, and tapped him on the shoulder, all within a couple of seconds, and all completely natural looking, completely appropriate, and completely effective. People who have met him always talk about his "charm" and "magnetism" – and of course he has a reputation for being attractive to women, even before he was the President.

Many men who aren't naturally "touchy" come to Love Systems thinking that they couldn't "get away with" normal physical progression. This is why I encourage guys to be the "creepy touchy guy" for a week or so. Sometimes you have to try to deliberately overshoot the mark to find out where the limits really are. You probably have much more freedom than you think.

With that in mind, let's take a look at each of the four phases of the Physical Progression Model.

1. Social Touch

Social Touch is the kind of touch that would be socially appropriate if the person you are touching is a complete stranger.

Generally, this kind of touch is on the elbow, shoulder, or hands. Common examples of social touch include:

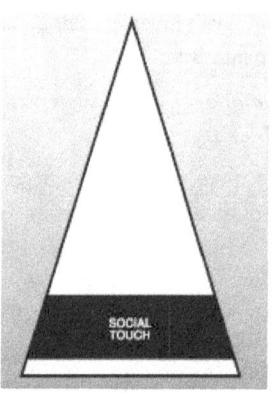

- Physically demonstrative handshakes (Bill Clinton example)
- Touching someone's arm or shoulder when you are making a point, showing a person something, or getting his or her attention
- High-fives
- "Games" like thumb-wrestling, hot hands, etc., that involve some touching

If you're confused about whether something qualifies as social touch, ask yourself: would you touch a man this way? If not, it's not social touch.

With Social Touch, you should touch everyone in a group who is close to you and treat everyone equally. No special attention for women, let alone for the woman you are specifically interested in.

Some Social Touch opportunities will almost always be there. For example, touching someone's arm or shoulder will always be a possibility. Other opportunities need to be created. For example, the handshake routine (in the Love Systems Routines Manual, Volume I) is explicitly designed in part to give you an opportunity to create and intensify Social Touch. That's the point of physical progression routines – to give you built-in opportunities to escalate your touching.

You can and should initiate social touch as early as possible in an interaction, usually within 30 seconds. This is important for establishing momentum to move forward into the next phase of the Physical Progression Model: Friendly Touch.

This is really important. Compare two approaches. Say I approach a group of strangers, and as part of my initial conversation, I'm using Social Touch. A few minutes later, I playfully put my arm around the woman I'm interested in for a second (Friendly Touch). It's not really awkward or worth anyone noticing or commenting on. It feels natural, as escalating physical touch always should.

Now, say I hadn't done any touching at first. When I try the same arm-around-her move a few minutes into the conversation, people will notice. It will seem "different" and people will feel the shift. It's not "natural" at all.

(On a more advanced note, this "natural" feeling is one reason why we teach men at our live training workshops to always be talking at the times when they are escalating physically (or logistically) so that they're drawing attention away from the escalation.)

2. Friendly Touch

Friendly Touch implies that you and the person you are touching are more than strangers. However, it doesn't necessarily imply romantic or sexual interest. For example:

Your arm around someone briefly

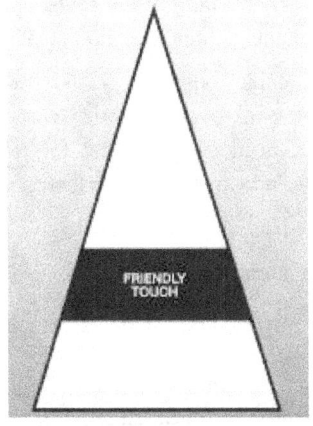

- Touch on the back

- Touch on the legs (in a seated position) but not the upper or inner thighs

- Fixing someone's hair

- Extended touching of someone's hands (Not holding hands – rather, the sort of hand touching if you were reading some one's palm)

- Holding her hand with an excuse (e.g., "come with me")

- Any kind of play fighting

- Hugs or "French-style" cheek kisses

- Role-playing touching

Often, things that qualify as Friendly Touch could also be Romantic Touch, depending on the context and duration. For example, if I put my arm around a female friend for a few seconds when I run into her, that's Friendly Touch. If I'm sitting on the couch with a woman with my arm around her for a half hour, that's Romantic Touch.

Friendly touch is a crucial bridge between Social Touch (available to anyone) and Romantic Touch (available only to potential romantic connections). It's great for testing her interest in you – does she reciprocate? Pull away? Intensify the connection?

3. **Romantic Touch**

Romantic touch is something that implies a connection beyond the "just friends" level. But don't assume anything. Until you've kissed her, she still has plausible deniability. She can be enjoying the feeling of Romantic Touch, enjoying the flirting, enjoying the sexual tension, and have absolutely no intention of proceeding further. (That's okay –

people who learn Love Systems get pretty good at getting beautiful women to change their minds.)

Examples of Romantic Touch include:

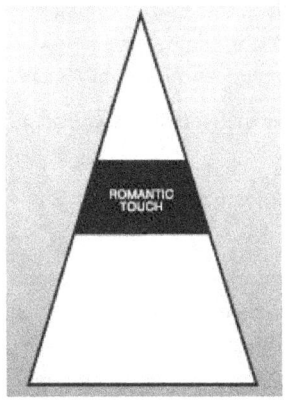

- Massages
- Stroking her hair
- Her sitting on your lap
- Holding hands
- Etc. (Note that Romantic Touch is not explicitly sexual.)

Kissing comes at the very end of Romantic Touch – and that's where plausible deniability ends. The makeout is an important signpost in the Physical Progression Model. Once she makes out with you, she's not flirting or being friendly, she's put herself out there. (But see the chapter on Kissing in the book Magic Bullets for some big pitfalls about kissing too soon or how it can dissipate sexual tension and kill your chances of advancing into Sexual Touch. It's not true that you should always go for the makeout as soon as you can.)

4. **Sexual Touch**

Sexual touch is the end zone of the physical model. It includes anything past kissing.

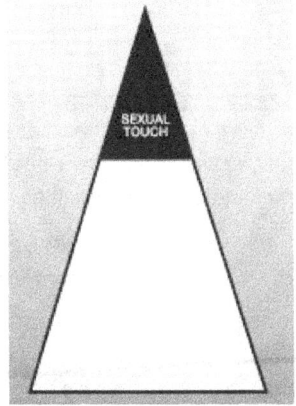

We're not going to teach you how to have sex in this book, but we are going to remind you of the potential obstacles and dead ends even once you get to this stage. Most of the time, these issues are emotional, not physical, and are dealt with in the chapter on Seduction in Magic Bullets.

The logistical progression model

A couple of years ago, I made the bold claim that "Advanced game is primarily about logistics." At the time, it was controversial. Now, of course, it's the conventional wisdom. But what does this actually mean?

"Logistics" is the social and physical context that you and a woman are in, and includes two critical questions:

> 1. Are her friends or other people associated with her around? (Social Logistics)

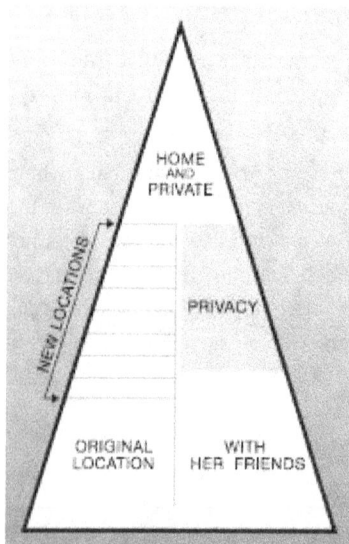

This only applies to her people. Your friends should be on your side and know what to do. If they don't, they could be great friends but they're not the people you should go out meeting women with. This is why lots of guys come to Love Systems live training workshops with their friends, or end up finding quality wingmen there.

Few women normally want to hook up while their friends look on. While advanced guys are good at changing this dynamic - something we talk about in our advanced material on female psychology – it's usually a safe assumption that you want to get her alone, where you can be more open with each other and where she might be less self-conscious.

> 2. How close are you to a place where sex could reasonably happen? (Location Logistics)

There's no sense getting her to want to have sex with you if you have nowhere to go. While many of the adventures I've had in VIP rooms, taxi cabs, and elsewhere have dramatically expanded my personal definition of "places where sex could reasonably happen," the standard assumption is that this means your house or hotel room. (Her place is okay too, but usually not as effective.) Other factors come into play logistically – for example, how much time she has, whether she has to get up in the morning, etc. - but these are the two most important.

USING LOGISTICS

Say you're on a date at a bar, you've been talking to her for a couple of hours, she's attracted, qualified, comfortable, and your conversation has become sexualized. Physically, you're all over each other. But... you live 45 minutes away, and she has a friend's birthday party she is supposed to be going to. Her friends are going to be angry with her if she doesn't turn up, and there's not enough time for her to come back to your place and still make it for her friend's birthday.

You, my friend, are not going home with her tonight. In fact, as we will see, it was counter-productive to advance so far Emotionally and Physically when your Logistics were so unfavorable. Hence, the importance of being able to quickly assess and manage logistics.

Because the Logistical Progression Model has two separate variables (Social and Location), it is a little bit more flexible than the stricter step-by-step Emotional and Physical systems.

In other words, you can do the two major steps in any order. You can get her alone first, and then take her home. Or you can take her home first and then her friends leave (or get distracted for long enough). Or you can do both at once – e.g., if you meet her when she's out with friends but the two of you leave together to go home.

Those are your basic plays, but there are also a bunch of intermediate steps available to you, depending on the situation. Use:

Social Logistics

- **Win her friends:** If you can't get her alone yet, try to get her friends on your side or at least neutral – either by getting them to communicate to her that it's okay for her to hook up, or by encouraging them to hook up themselves. The latter option is another reason why good wingmen are so valuable.

Location Logistics

- **In-venue moves:** These are the easiest moves to make. In a shopping mall, for example, you can move a woman to a seated area or to a coffee shop. In-venue moves are helpful for building momentum toward bigger moves later. Moreover, as we'll see below, location moves generally help you Emotionally and Logistically.

- **Intermediate moves:** You have more options than "stay where you are" or "go home." You also can take her, with her friends if necessary, to one or more different venues. Ideally these should trend geographically toward home. For example, you might meet a woman at a restaurant, and then suggest grabbing a drink – at a place that is conveniently near where you live, building momentum for the big move to your place later on.

- **Reset / "Time Bridge":** Finally, there's the common logistical tool of the phone number exchange. Usually, when you see her again, you can plan the logistics so that she'll be alone and your date will naturally end at or near home. Given that most people are relatively busy when you meet them in the daytime, this is probably the most frequent way you'll logistically escalate in daytime dating. These location tools are especially effective when you use little moves to create momentum. She's more likely to come home with you if she's already used to following your lead as you walked with her down the street, took her a to coffee shop, went on a date with her in a bar, took her to a great dessert place near where you live, and so on.

Putting it all together – Implications

One of the reasons the Love Systems Triad has been so successful is because it's fairly easy to learn while its implications can be very advanced and sophisticated.

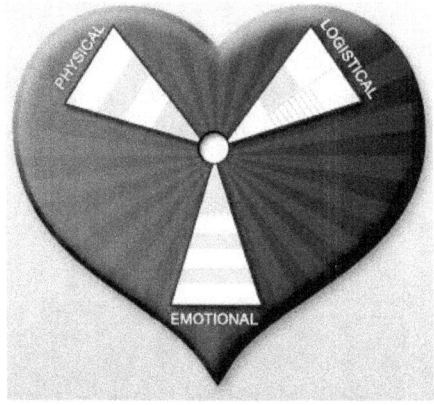

Because everyone is unique, some implications may be more important to your style than others. We've learned that most people will do better if they discover the most important implications "naturally" through using the Love Systems Triad, as opposed to trying to memorize them. But here are a few important ones to get you started:

1. Always be moving toward the center.

If it doesn't advance you emotionally, physically, or logistically, then don't do it. Succeeding with beautiful women is often about what you don't do as opposed to what you actually do. Taking the useless extra stuff out of your game should already improve your results.

So - whenever you feel stuck – move toward the center.

2. Get momentum on your side – don't let it work against you.

You can't stay too long in any phase of any part of the Triad forever. It will bore or frustrate most women. For example, even if you had a great three hours meeting a woman at a party and you made it all the way to the Comfort phase emotionally and to Romantic touch physically, but the next two weeks consisted of both of you unluckily leaving messages on each other's voicemail, your failure to move forward Logistically means you will lose momentum, and, eventually, her interest. Lack of momentum can work against you through no fault of your own.

Momentum can also work for you. Each phase that you can smoothly pass through builds up your momentum for the next one. When a woman talks about sleeping with you and says, "it just happened," that's momentum at work.

By the way, this is where the more advanced concepts of investment and social momentum (otherwise outside the scope of this chapter) come into play. If you can get her to invest in you – by, say, following you around the bar, or waiting while you're on the phone, or really doing anything that you ask her to do – that builds social momentum that can be applied (in order of impact) logistically, physically, or emotionally.

3. Progress in sync.

Have you ever gotten a woman all hot and bothered, taken her home, and been near the finish line when she says "stop... too fast... why do you like me?" You let the emotional lag behind the physical and logistical – probably in this case it was an issue with Qualification.

Or have you ever had a date like my "let's just be friends" disaster I talked about earlier - where everything went well emotionally and logistically, but I got rejected because I was nowhere physically?

Don't make avoidable mistakes. Don't let any dimension lag way behind.

4. There are shortcuts if you learn the relationships between specific points on the Triad.

A much more advanced and multi-dimensional implication – and one we're not going to fully cover here but that I want to put in your head so you can recognize it when it happens – is that there are specific relationships between the three dimensions. The three models are not isolated and separate.

For example, the very act of moving up the first two steps on the Physical Progression Model will help you emotionally. Study after study has shown that women are more apt to be sexually and romantically interested in men when there is (appropriate) touching as a subtext to their conversation. This actually applies to non-romantic interactions as well.

Some other examples:

- *Location moves [Logistics] help you progress emotionally.* The more contexts in which she sees herself with you, the better she will feel she knows you. For example, a date that hits three places for an hour each is much better than a date that stays in one place for three hours.

- *If you get to Romantic Touch on the Physical Progression Model, you've already accomplished Attraction on the Emotional Progression Model, whether you know it or not.* Trying to attract a woman who is already attracted is worse than pointless; it's counter-productive.

- *Don't start Comfort without hitting Friendly Touch.* Building deep comfort when there is no physical conversation is the easiest way to get her to say: "Let's Just Be Friends."

- *Don't get into Sexual Touch unless you are in a Logistical (and Emotional) position to take advantage of it.* This can dissipate sexual tension, and actually reduce the chances of seeing her again if you don't close the deal that night.

Nick Savoy

www.lovesystems.com/savoy

Love Systems triad in daytime dating

Now that you understand the Love Systems Triad, let's look at how we can apply this to daytime dating. Although situations will vary widely, this is the typical sort of game plan you want to have:

1. Approach and Transition – 30 seconds

2. Attract & Qualify – 1-10 minutes

3. Organize a date (with specific time and place)

4. Date – 2-3 hours

Don't treat this like a rigid schematic for all the women you meet. Every situation and every woman is slightly different. But the above is a good guideline to stick to for the majority of women you approach in the daytime.

The first part is approaching her and transitioning into a full conversation. Once you've done that, you want to build Attraction and Qualification with her for up to around 10 minutes. At the end of that conversation, you want to ask her out. If she says yes, you should establish a rough time and place to have a date with her (rather than simply taking her number and following up later – which as we'll see in Logistical Progression, can lead to a lot of women giving you their phone number but not following through).

Don't worry too much about Physical Progression in the first instance of meeting her in the daytime. It's true that in a bar or club, it can be advantageous to get relatively physical as soon as you start talking to her. But in the daytime, it's less socially acceptable to do so and you might creep her out if you try. As a rule, definitely avoid going into Romantic Touch until you're on a date with her, and possibly even wait until then to go into Friendly Touch (though this will vary a little depending how friendly the woman is when you meet her).

Once you're on a date with her, you should spend a few hours with her and if things go well, either take things further (for example, asking her to come back to your place) or ending the date with an expectation that you'll see each other again.

This might seem overwhelming to do all this right now, but as you read further into this book, the individual steps and how you make them happen will become clearer to you.

PART II
EMOTIONAL PROGRESSION

Chapter 5: Approaching

What is approaching?

Approaching is the first stage of Emotional Progression and simply means starting a conversation with a woman. It's also one of the stages that men tend to find the most intimidating because it naturally involves a chance of rejection.

Have you ever been to a bar early in the evening when it's quiet and noticed how groups of people don't really mingle and talk to each other? There are always a few beautiful women sitting around but no one is approaching them. Why? Because no one wants to be the first guy to do it.

If you do pluck up the courage to go have a five minute conversation with a couple of beautiful women, suddenly you open the floodgates and you'll notice other men approaching them immediately after you. Seeing you do it has given them permission to do it themselves.

In most daytime situations, you have to learn to be that first guy: to give yourself permission. Seeing other people doing daytime approaches is rare (which is why the live workshops are so useful). Most people, when they look around in daytime situations and see strangers not talking to each other (the classic example is on a subway or bus), think, "Well, if no one else is doing it, I probably shouldn't either." You have to fight these thoughts and be willing to do what every other guy is thinking of doing but doesn't have the courage to.

These are some of the things that went through my head years ago when I did my first few approaches on women I didn't know (what we call "cold approaches"):

- She is going to think I'm weird

- She is going to tell me to get lost

- She is out of my league

- Everyone is going to look at me

- I am going to feel silly

Be willing to challenge these assumptions every time you feel them. It's true that these thoughts and emotions can cause discomfort for a few minutes, but you'll prefer them to the much longer-lasting feeling of regret you'll experience for the next few hours, days or weeks if you don't approach a woman you like.

Approaching in daytime dating

There are a few important differences to approaching women in the daytime as opposed to doing so at night in a bar or club.

- The women you approach will often be busy or on their way somewhere when you meet them.

You won't always have a chance to spend lots of time with them (and run through the whole Love Systems Triad model) in the first instance, but will typically have to arrange to meet her again at another time (i.e. set up a date).

- Women will more often be alone than they would in a nightclub or bar.

This means you don't need to think about entertaining a group and impressing all of her friends as much, but can focus on connecting with her individually.

- Women are approached far less often in the daytime than at night.

For this reason, women tend to be a lot more impressed when you approach them in the daytime, and the process of building an interaction can often seem easier than at night.

Now let's take a look at exactly how to approach a woman you find attractive in the daytime. We're going to cover the main verbal and non-verbal elements of an approach, and then some more advanced considerations.

Verbal elements of the approach

The simplest, easiest, and most powerful way you can approach a woman in the daytime is use what we call a "direct approach," which means expressing some immediate physical interest in her in order to begin a conversation. It does not mean asking her out immediately, asking for a phone number, or telling her you want to sleep with her, but rather paying her a compliment and expressing in some way that you want to have a conversation with her.

Historically in the field of seduction, there's been a lot of discussion on the benefits of direct versus "indirect approaches," where your physical interest in her is masked and a conversation begins through means of a ruse or gambit. It's my personal preference to use direct approaches most of the time for daytime dating, and this is what I've found to be the most effective for most daytime environments. However, we will also take a look at indirect approaches after this.

The structure of a good direct approach on a woman looks like this:

[Get her attention] + [Social Calibration] + [Compliment]

You have to get her attention so she listens to what you are about to say; the meat of which will be the compliment. The Social Calibration part is about adjusting to whatever situation you're both in, to make her feel more comfortable and demonstrate some social intelligence (which we'll talk more about in Attraction later).

Some examples are:

> *Excuse me, I just saw you walking past, and I had to come tell you that you look absolutely beautiful.*
>
> *Excuse me, I just saw you sitting there, and I wanted to come tell you that you look incredible.*
>
> *Hi, I saw you from across the room and I thought you looked gorgeous. I wanted to come introduce myself.*

You can play with these a little bit, and you should. Putting your own spin on the opening line is important to inject your own personality into it, to show a bit of the real you, and also to ensure that you enjoy the process of talking to women. At the start, however, feel free to use the lines above verbatim until you feel comfortable ad libbing and expressing how you genuinely feel moment to moment for each woman you see.

Social Calibration

The Social Calibration part of your opening line is the "I saw you walking past/sitting there/standing there" (or any other information on what you saw her doing). This element helps to ground what is about to follow in your opening line. If you leave out the Social Calibration, it can appear a bit abrupt to run up to a woman and just exclaim, "You're gorgeous!"

You can vary the Social Calibration. It doesn't always have to be about her; it can be about what you're doing too.

Here are some other examples:

> I was just over there with my friends and couldn't help but notice you...
>
> My friend and I saw you standing there...

I'm late to a meeting, and I probably shouldn't be stopping, but I just saw you...

Compliment

The compliment should demonstrate an explicit physical interest in her attractiveness. Don't for example, say things like "you have great shoes" or "I like your scarf" (or at least, don't say these things alone) otherwise she might misconstrue you to be interested in having a conversation about fashion. You want to communicate in some explicit way that you find her physically attractive first, and then if you want you can comment on more specific things in her style.

I often start with something fairly generic, for example "I think you look gorgeous," but then add on something a little more specific.

For example:

> *I really like your sense of style.*
>
> *The way you carry yourself just reeks of self-confidence. I like that.*
>
> *Something about the way your hair is done caught my eye. It's striking.*

By complimenting something specific about her, you make her feel more special and not just a random woman you approached (in this way, you've actually begun a little Qualification). Also, if you're going to use a specific compliment, focus on something within her control like her style, her hair or her body language (the way she stands, sits or walks for example), rather than characteristics she can't control, like her eye colour or height.

Non-verbal elements of the approach

Your style, your body language and your speech are all going to have a big impact on how well your direct approaches work. It's important to bear the following in mind:

- **Look your best.** Dress stylishly, fix your hair and be clean. Don't walk out of the house looking your worst and thinking it doesn't matter. You might see the most beautiful woman you've ever seen and then forever regret that you had a mustard stain on your white shirt.

- **Carry yourself well.** Keep your head up, your shoulders back and your chest pushed forwards. Don't look at the ground when you're walking. Don't slouch when you're sitting.

- **Speak confidently.** Take the time to figure out exactly what you're going to say and then say it clearly and concisely. Talking too softly or talking excessively demonstrates a lack of confidence in what you are saying.

- **Slow down and pause.** Most guys deliver their approach too fast. Slow down the pace of your opening words: try pausing for a few seconds after you get her attention with the "excuse me" and also after you finish delivering the compliment (and just before you ask her name). In those brief pauses, maintain strong eye contact with her and smile. The pausing element alone will skyrocket the success of your approaches (but honestly, you won't believe me until you try it to see what I mean). Try a three-second pause (I know it sounds like a long time) in your opening line and see how it changes the dynamic.

Strong body language and confidence in your speech are easier to model from real life than they are to understand from a written book. Have a look at men who are confident and observe how they move, stand, gesticulate and speak. The key people to look at are those with high status; for example, CEOs, celebrities and other men that you see women being very attracted to.

Approach logistics

In order to start a conversation with a woman, you have to be able to get her attention in the most effective way possible. That is why the "Excuse me" part of the approach is important – to ensure that she listens to the rest of what you are about to say.

For example, for women standing on the street or sitting on a park bench, it's not too difficult to get their attention. You just go up to them and deliver your approach. For women who are seated down, if they respond well to your initial approach and you can get into conversation with them, you need to sit down with them – just ask "Do you mind if I join you for a minute?"

For women who are walking past you on the street, however, it can be a little bit more involved. They're on their way somewhere, so you have to work a little harder to get their attention. I've discovered through years of trial and improvement that the best thing is to approach them from behind and to the side a little, touch them lightly on the arm and then deliver your approach as you (and hopefully her) stop moving. Even if I see her walking towards me, I will let her pass and then turn around to approach her from behind. Here's a diagram to explain further:

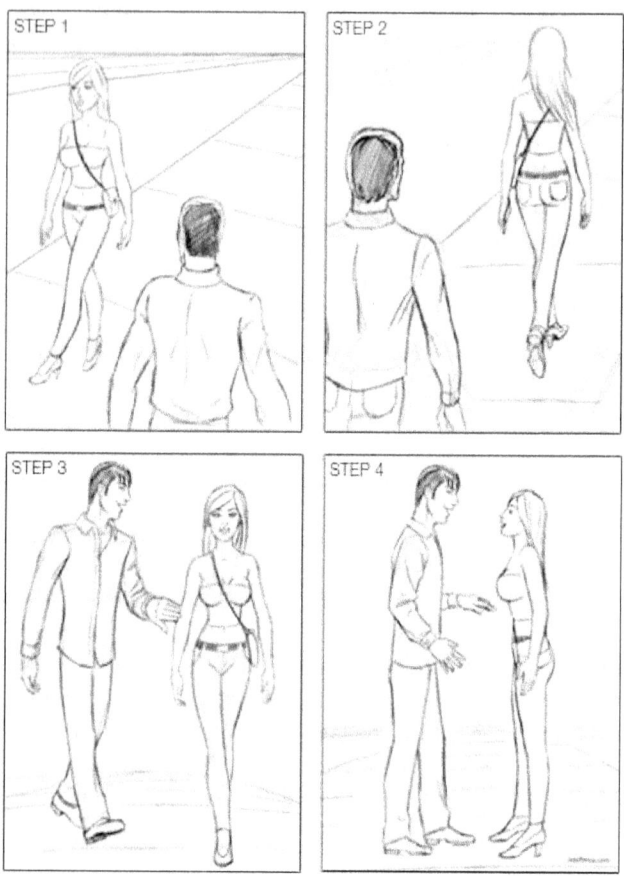

Illustrations by Jess Perna, JessPerna.com

To some people it sounds counterintuitive to approach from behind. But if you approach them from the front as they walk towards you, it can appear as if you're trying to sell something to them, especially in big cities which are rife with street sellers. On the other hand, if you approach from behind and lightly touch a woman on the arm, it's almost as if an old friend must have seen her walking past and wanted to say hello. Of course when she turns around and discovers that it's a stranger, that's your chance to deliver a good approach and flatter her.

If you find that a woman doesn't stop moving as you touch her and say your opening line, don't continue moving with her – to do so would look creepy. Stop dead in your tracks and project your voice until she stops. If she stops, you can close the distance as you keep talking to her. If she doesn't stop, don't worry. Maybe she was too busy, maybe your body language was off, but regardless, there are plenty more women you can approach.

To better understand approach logistics and see daytime approaches in action, check out the Love Systems Youtube channel where you can see hidden camera footage of me approaching women:

youtube.com/lovesystems

Advanced considerations

Once you start doing a lot of daytime approaches, you'll probably notice a few situations that are a little more challenging, for example, approaching a woman when she's walking with a friend or group of friends. If you're not comfortable approaching a woman by herself, then don't worry too much about the more difficult situations right now. Focus on making the verbal and non-verbal elements of your approaching strong before you do so.

Challenging situations are actually really good opportunities to demonstrate your social intelligence (which as we'll see in the Attraction chapter is very attractive to a woman). Here are some tips for dealing with some of the more common ones:

- If she is with a friend, acknowledge the friend politely after you've started the conversation. If you are being direct, after you've approached the woman you want, say, "You're very lovely too, but I just have a thing for XYZ [for example, brunettes, tall girls, girls in red dresses]" to the friend. Then make sure to get the friend involved in whatever conversations you're having.

- If you moved a large distance or diverted from your original path of walking to talk to her, tell her, for example, "Excuse me, I was just eating my lunch over there when I saw you sitting here – you looked so beautiful and charming. I had to come say hello."

- If she looks startled as you start talking, say, "I'm sorry, I didn't mean to startle you! I just had to come over and tell you..." before you launch into your normal approach.

- If it's really crowded where she is, consider waiting a little until there's more space to approach her. The more people she has bustling by her, the more apprehensive she is going to be when you approach her, so it might be worth waiting until she is in an area that isn't as crowded.

If you are anything like me when I first started approaching women in the daytime, you will make all sorts of excuses to not approach a woman. You will claim you can't because she is with friends, she looks busy or she looks mean. As a friend of mine once told me, "There are always a hundred reasons not to approach her, and only one reason why you should."

Here's a good example of approaching in a situation where most men wouldn't have – the key was just to be socially intelligent. I recently dated a young model whom I'm met while she was out shopping with her mother. I approached both of them, started talking to the mother, commenting on how beautiful her daughter was and how she had done well to raise her. After introducing myself (first to the mother and then the daughter), I turned to the daughter and found out a little bit more about her. I made sure to keep the mother engaged in conversation from time to time so that she didn't feel awkward. By approaching the mother first – who had the power in the social situation – and complimenting her for raising her daughter well, I had shown high social intelligence. After that it was down to me to have an interesting conversation with both of them.

Indirect approaches

Although using a direct approach is my personal preference, I've had some clients that never found it comfortable to be so upfront about their physical interest in a woman. For these guys, they feel much more comfortable starting an innocuous conversation with a woman about what she's listening to on her iPod, the book she's reading, or something else going on in the situation around them.

It's always worth experimenting and persisting for a while with direct approaches if you've never tried them, but if they are really not your thing then by all means, use indirect approaches.

There are various types of indirect approach such as opinion, situational, and functional. The information on when and how to use these approaches has already been covered in great detail in Magic Bulets and there's no point re-inventing the wheel here. But let's look at a couple of factors that you should take into consideration when using indirect approaches in daytime dating.

First, because women are generally in a less social mindset in the daytime (often on their way to meetings, on lunch breaks etc.) than at night, you have to be careful to ground your approach appropriately to the situation you're in. When you're in a bar, you can ask a woman her opinion on something as if you had just been having a conversation with a friend about it (because it's a social context, it's not beyond the realm of normality to start talking to people around you about random things).

But if you stop a woman on the street and ask for her opinion on something, she will think, "Why is he asking me, instead of the dozens of other women walking past?" On the other hand, if you're in a clothes store and ask for an opinion on some clothes, it would be grounded to the context and make more sense.

Second, how distracted she is will affect how successful an indirect approach is. For example, a functional approach such as, "Do you have a light?" or "Do you know where the nearest Starbucks is?" might work for a woman standing somewhere by herself or perhaps walking slowly. But a woman in a rush, carrying lots of bags or frantically browsing clothes on a discount rack is probably going to invest much less in an indirect conversation. In such cases, it might be hard to successfully approach her anyway, but if you're going to try it, your best shot is to be direct.

Here are some more examples of indirect approaches:

> *What are you listening to on your iPod? I'm really bored of my playlist at the moment.*
>
> *I've heard that book is really good. If I could read, I'd totally buy it. How are you enjoying it?*
>
> *This subway is so crowded. If I faint, will you catch me?*
>
> *Wow, your laptop is so much cooler than mine. I'm jealous. I totally have laptop envy right now.*
>
> *You're not from around here, are you?*

How to make a direct approach work

Here are the fundamental things to be aware of when using a direct approach.

1. Have strong body language

If you slouch, place your hands in a supplicating position (for example, with your palms facing up) or avoid eye contact, she will immediately think you are a low status man. Concentrate on pushing your chest out, keeping your shoulders back, holding your head high and moving at a slow pace at all times – especially when you are delivering the approach.

2. Have strong speech

The most important things in your speech are to slow it down and include pauses. If you rush the whole approach out immediately, it sounds like you're afraid she is going to run away before you have a chance to finish. Include pauses for dramatic effect between parts of the approach, for example, "Excuse me... [pause] I just saw you walking past... [pause] and I had to come tell you... [pause] your outfit is incredible." Also, don't raise your voice at the end of the sentence – it sounds like you are supplicating if you do.

3. Compliment something specific

It's very easy to tell a woman she's beautiful but it takes a high status man to notice the specifics of what is attractive about her. A man that pays attention to detail in the first few seconds is normally a man that pays attention to her in bed. You will generally do best to compliment a woman on her style, her hair or her body language. Use unusual words that most men probably wouldn't think of using in a compliment, for example, "elegant", "graceful" or "alluring".

Here are some specific examples:

> *"You have an incredible style. It's clear that you have good taste and a sense of coordination."*
>
> *"I love the way your hair just cascades off your head like that. It's so alluring.*
>
> *"You carry yourself with such confidence, and yet without any hint of arrogance."*

4. Show that you have high standards

In addition to making the compliment specific, you can also show high status by incidentally mentioning your standards. For example, after she responds to the initial compliment you could say, "Seriously, it's so rare where I'm from to see a woman with this kind of style; you have something unique about you that most women don't have."

By pointing out that most women you meet don't have the quality that you've complimented her for, you're showing that you're able to meet a lot of women but that most of them – the average ones – hold no interest for you. You're after something special, and therefore you are unlike the average guy.

5. Show that you want more than just looks

The ultimate goal of the approach is not to impress her or to begin the process of seduction. The ultimate goal is to start a conversation in order to find out whether you want to get to know her better or not. This is a mindset that most guys don't ever consider adopting; they've already decided just from the way she looks that they want to sleep with her. A man with abundance and real choice in his life wants much more.

Set the tone that you started the conversation with her because she's physically attractive, but you want to find out more to see if she is your type. I often tag, "I had to come and find out some more about you," into the approach or the first minute of conversation. For example, "Excuse me, I saw you walking past and I loved your style. I wanted to come and find out some more about you."

Contrast this with, "You're beautiful. I had to come and ask you out on a date," which shows that you're willing to commit your precious time just on the basis of her being good looking. That's not a trait of the high status man.

6. Be ready to lead the conversation on after the approach

Most guys expect a direct approach to make a woman magically jump you or exclaim, "Wow, you're so brave! Take my number!" after delivering it. But the ideal and most common response is simply her being pleasantly surprised and saying, "Thank you." After this, it is still down to you to lead the conversation and have an attractive interaction.

You can take it where you want after the approach. I tend to ask a few questions to figure out what the woman's personality and lifestyle is like and whether she's someone I want to get to know better. I might also get some banter going by making a few situational jokes. The important thing is to have some follow-up immediately after the approach, otherwise you will get just a "Thank you," and the woman will turn back to whatever she was doing.

7. *Believe that she is going to respond positively*

This is a hard one. Approaches work best when you believe they are going to work – because your body language and speech are aligned in a way conducive to it working. That belief only truly comes when you have enough positive reference experiences of it working.

So realize that the first ten, fifty or hundred times you try it, it might be tough. But at some point you will get into a few really good conversations and start to see it working. At this point, you have good reference experiences and you will feel more confident to approach a woman directly.

Chapter summary

- The basic structure of a direct daytime approach is:
  [Get her attention] + [Social Calibration] + [Compliment].

- In addition to the verbal elements, it's important to focus on non-verbal elements in your approach such as your style, your body language and your speech.

- For a woman walking past you, let her walk past and then double back, catch up to her and touch her lightly on the arm to deliver your approach. For a woman seated down, approach her, and then if she responds well, ask her if you can join her for a minute.

- If you try direct approaches and you really can't get used to them, you can try in direct approaches. However, for these to work, you'll need to focus on approaching women in static settings and getting into an appropriate position where you could start a seemingly innocuous conversation.

Chapter 6: Transitioning

After you approach a woman and she responds, you need to begin a bigger conversation. Transitioning is the second stage of Emotional Progression and achieves this.

In the daytime, particularly if you've used a direct approach, transitioning is very easy. It's often as simple as introducing yourself, exchanging names and shaking the woman's hand.

Although it sounds simple, it is a very important step. By introducing yourself, you communicate to her in a socially intelligent way, "We're about to have a conversation," which will allow you to start talking and ask about multiple topics. Also, shaking her hand is a form of Social Touch, which begins Physical Progression (covered in detail later on).

If a woman responds really well to your initial approach, this exchange of names and handshake is normally all you need. However, if she doesn't respond so well and doesn't look too impressed, it might help to use a stronger transition.

In such cases, re-emphasize what you originally said and then tangent into something that you noticed about her or some related topic. What you tangent onto should demonstrate something interesting about you, or call attention to something of interest about her. Here are some examples:

> *No really, there are a lot of good-looking girls in this city, but you have a unique style. I'm guessing that you do something creative for a living or in your spare time?*

> *I meant what I said about the way you carry yourself. You really do have a graceful walk. I'm wondering whether you're a dancer or have had some kind of dance training before?*

Really, you do have an interesting look – very different from most of the women I meet in this city. I'm guessing you're not from around here?

Notice in these examples there's an implicit sense that you have some relevant experience in those things you call attention to. For example, by (hopefully correctly) guessing about her dance training, it shows that you've either dated dancers before, you have friends who are dancers, or you've worked in the industry yourself. By enquiring about her creativity, you're giving her an opportunity to talk about something she is probably passionate about. By pointing out that she's "different from most of the women you've met in this city," you're demonstrating that you're not short of choice for women in your love life, but maybe you're picky.

Using stronger transitions like these give a woman a window into what else you have to offer. A lot of this will become clearer as we go through the next chapter on Attraction and talk about how you have to offer "social value" to a woman.

Forming the Approach Habit

By , Keychain Love Systems instructor

"We are what we repeatedly do. Excellence then, is not an act, but a habit." - Aristotle

Most of us are awake and moving about the world during the day far more than at night. We shop, we work, we eat and we travel. For those of us who live in or near a populated area like a city, there are lots of opportunities to meet beautiful women in the daytime.

When I first arrived at university, I would go out at night with my friends to meet girls. Perhaps three or four times a week we would hit the club and spend hours approaching groups of women and hitting on them. Later, after finding Love Systems and being armed with new knowledge, I would increase this practice and often go alone to bars and clubs to meet new people and exercise my social muscle. I felt nervous at first but after a couple of approaches in an evening this feeling would fade. After that, it was as if my motor was running; I'd have a sense of flow, excitement and social lubrication. After those initial nervous conversations, I felt acclimatized to approaching strangers and could work on other aspects of my dating skill beyond the initial approach.

Inevitably, the night would end, with all its various ups and downs. Lo and behold, the next time I went out to the bar, that fear of approach was once again back to bother me.

Going out specifically to talk to and meet new women is great for practicing core aspects of your dating skills but something most people do not practice as intensely is overcoming that initial reluctance to approach, often referred to as "approach anxiety". This is simply because after a couple of interactions, this feeling fades. After that initial warm-up period, we usually find the social motor is running, we're having fun and approaching without too much worry, but it doesn't last. Every time we go out, this feeling tends to crop up and needs to be overcome again.

It is generally accepted that this is just the way it must be. The oft-prescribed solution is to burn through some warm-up approaches to get in the right mood. But what if it was possible to greatly minimize that feeling of nervousness over time so that you could generate the momentum to approach at any time you wished without the need to warm up? What if there was a way to form a habit of approaching beautiful girls?

Picture the scene: you're shopping for groceries, on public transport or walking down the street and you see a beautiful girl. You don't have the advantage of the mental run-up from which you can make a conscious decision to practice your dating skills today, you have no friends nearby to spur you on and you can't just burn through two or three approaches to get on a roll and then approach this girl. You're just going about your daily life and bam, she appears! Do you approach? Can you approach?

The First Hot Girl

"Approach the first hot girl you see every day. It will change your life."

- Sasha

Begin an interaction with a stranger, preferably a beautiful woman, everyday. This begins to form an approach habit – the daily habit of initiating conversation with someone from cold. Over time, this habit can become so ingrained that it will actually feel strange not to approach a hot girl. The energy that you previously experienced as fear and panic will morph into excitement, playfulness and enjoyment.

This will not only help you greatly minimize approach anxiety, but the daily routine will have you meeting more girls than ever before.

Training Your Eye

Forming the approach habit will also go a long way towards training your eye to become aware of the opportunities already present in your surroundings. If you know you need to approach at least one girl in your lunch break for instance, you get good at noticing the attractive girls all around you.

It is not unusual, a week or so into this, for people to say things along the lines of, "I never realized there were so many hot girls around here!" Sometimes we can work and live in an area for years without realizing the opportunities all around us.

Don't Run the Perfect Approach

Don't worry about running the perfect approach in every one of these interactions. At first, don't even worry about continuing the conversation. If you are short on time, just make your daily interaction a quick one. Remember, we are forming the approach habit. For this purpose, it is more important at first to approach than to necessarily take it anywhere. Don't let the pressure of "What do I say next?" and "What if...?" questions dissuade you from taking action.

When you spot that girl, and you get that feeling of "I should/could/can/want to approach her," go talk to her. If it lasts ten seconds or ten minutes, it doesn't matter – just approach. Form the approach habit.

Avoid Burnout

"Habit is habit and not to be flung out of the window by any man, but coaxed downstairs a step at a time."

- Mark Twain

It's much like joining a gym. In the first flush of enthusiasm and novelty, the temptation is to go very frequently and stay for hours, working really hard. But continue down this road and it is very likely you'll experience burn out. You will lose your motivation and weeks will go by before you darken the gym door again (if at all!). It is much more sensible (and healthy) to do shorter workouts and ration that drive for the long-haul health benefits of regular exercise.

Consider this point when embarking on your mission to form the approach habit. One a day for a month is far better than ten in two days, burning out and doing nothing for the rest of the month.

Find Your Window

Look at your lifestyle, find the window of time where you can make your daily approach and stick to it. For me, I had a long commute, so I would use the train journey and approach at least one girl on the way into London and one on the way out of London. For you, your lunch break might be an ideal time. Whatever it is, find your window.

Scale It Up

It can feel more challenging to approach during the day without having a friend (a "wingman") there to encourage you.

If you're alone and feeling nervous, just take off some pressure. Scale the opener you use – if you're petrified, you don't have to start direct and ballsy, start more situational and low-key. For example, a functional approach such as, "Excuse me, do you know if there's a Starbucks around here?" is much easier to muster the courage to deliver than, "I saw you from across the street and I just had to come say hi, because I think you're gorgeous!" If you gradually scale up your material, just as you would add weight to your bench press routine, you will be able to deliver the latter approach with ease and enthusiasm.

Fashion

If you're going to form this habit, be ready. Always leave the house dressed well, whatever that means for your lifestyle. Throw out your bad clothes so you won't be tempted to wear them – don't let the fact that you're dressed badly be an excuse to not approach. Dressing well has a positive impact on your interactions with everyone in your life.

Wingman/Mentor

Your daily approaches should be done solo for maximum growth, but it can help to have a wingman or accountability buddy who will check in with you every day to make sure you've done your approach. This added motivation can give you the kick start you need to start forming the habit.

Conclusion

Does this mean you shouldn't go out for concentrated periods of time specifically to meet women? No!

Working on your dating skill in focused periods like this is great for getting those skills tight – perhaps your Attraction phase needs tweaking or your comfort phase lacks connection. Go out, hit the streets, shopping malls and bookstores and do a ton of approaches. The trick is to combine this with daily approaching to build and sustain the approach habit. Do this and you'll go a long way towards achieving your relationship goals.

I often think of the ability to approach as a muscle. For every approach you make, you grow that muscle. For every approach you back out of, you weaken it.

Make those approaches, build your courage. The results may very well astound you.

Good luck!

Keychain

www.lovesystems.com/keychain

Chapter 7: Attraction

What is attraction?

Once you've approached a woman and transitioned into a conversation with her, Attraction is the next phase you should concentrate on. Attraction is where a woman begins to think of you as someone she could potentially sleep with, rather than just as a friend or a stranger.

To explain how Attraction works, we use the concept of value. Value is what makes something desirable. Value for men and women is different. Generally speaking, women are more interested in men for social value and men are more interested in women for physical value during the Attraction phase. That is a vital piece of knowledge you need to embrace in understanding how to get better with women. So let me repeat that: women are more interested in men for our social value, where we are more interested in women for their physical value.

The effects of this can be seen all over the world in lots of different and common situations. For example, female employees often feel some attraction for their boss, regardless of how physically good looking he is. Women are often attracted to celebrities, regardless of how obnoxious they can sometimes be. Finally, if you look at a men's magazine like askmen.com, you'll notice that there are lists of "the world's most beautiful women" but that the equivalent list for men typically comprises "the world's most socially influential men." In short, society prizes women for their beauty, and men for their social capability. Your task then, when you first meet a woman, is to demonstrate that you have high social value.

Your social value as a man is determined by a lot of different things, but there are a few things that women specifically look for (even if unconsciously) to estimate your social value when they first meet you. For example, your general confidence, your sense of humor and how well you seem to get along with other people around you. We call these things attraction switches (also known as Demonstrations of Higher Value or DHVs), which we'll go into more details of shortly.

You need to show social value to a woman when you meet her by using these attraction switches. If you are failing to attract women in your life, it is very likely because you are not using these switches.

You might be wondering at this stage, exactly what do you say to a woman or what do you talk about to make her interested in you? In the Conversation Mapping chapter, we'll go through the specifics of how you structure a typical daytime dating conversation, but first of all we need to go through the fundamentals of Attraction and Qualification. As you learn more about these topics, we'll be able to tie them together into having an initial, attractive conversation with a woman that potentially results in a date with her.

Attraction in daytime dating

Attraction building in the daytime needs to be executed with some adjustments to how you might do it in a nightclub or bar.

- Attraction in the daytime is generally shorter than it would be at night, only taking approximately 1-10 minutes (in this book I'll generally refer to a "five minute conversation" as an approximation).

Because you've approached her in a situation where she doesn't normally get approached (or at least with far less frequency than she does at night), your value is already very high and you need to do less work to build her attraction.

- You don't need to do much Disqualification (a technique to feign disinterest or ambivalence towards a woman) in the daytime.

If fact, disqualifying too much can actually hurt your chances with a woman you meet in the daytime – particularly if you won her over in the first place with a direct approach. A bit of light teasing can be good, but avoid the stronger disqualifiers.

- It's important to show some Passion (whether that's for your job, hobbies or any other interest you have in life) when you meet a woman in the daytime, and ideally, to find common passions between you.

Although Passion is a good value to show to a woman regardless of where you meet her, in the daytime in particular, it's something that will help her become attracted to you very quickly. Compare this with a nightclub, where it could be considered more important to be seen as a challenge before talking about your passions. For this reason, Magic Bullets readers will note the addition of a Passion attraction switch in this chapter in place of the Challenging attraction switch. That's not to say that both are not important when you meet a woman, but simply to help you focus on what's most important for those first few minutes in the daytime.

Snapshot theory

As you get used to using the attraction switches, it's easy to get carried away and end up trying too hard to impress a woman or to reveal more about yourself than is necessary.

It can actually be very unattractive for a woman to know everything about you. Particularly when you have just approached her in the daytime, she doesn't need to know all the details of why she should be interested in you, just that you could be the sort of man she could spend more time with. This element of mystery is very intriguing to a woman.

For this reason, it's important to give her a snapshot picture of yourself by demonstrating as many of the different attraction switches as possible, without relying on any one too much. Think about presenting yourself as a well-rounded character instead of a guy who is just a funny guy or just a guy who is passionate about music for example.

When we get to the Conversation Mapping chapter, you'll see how it's important not to dwell on any one conversation topic too long, even if the both of you have an avid interest in it. The key is simply to show her as attractive an overall snapshot of yourself as possible.

Now let's take a look at the 8 attraction switches in more detail.

The attraction switches

1. Appearance

Although the way a man looks isn't as important in determining attraction for a woman as the way a woman looks to a man, it certainly isn't going to hurt your chances to make yourself look as good as possible.

We can control our appearance a lot more than most people think. It's not just about your bone structure or your body shape: your style, your body language and the way you speak all affect how attractive a woman perceives you as. If you act like a confident, strong, attractive man, you'll find women start to refer to you as handsome a lot more often.

Being out in the daytime is not an excuse to dress sloppily. You have no idea when a beautiful woman might walk by you – it might happen when you pop out of the house for a few minutes to buy groceries. So be ready and make sure you look decent whenever you leave the house.

Having good style means conveying a particular identity. Are you trying to convey to others that you are an entrepreneur, a creative type, or a college student for example? Have in mind the image you'd like to present to women and get clothes and accessories to represent that as well as possible.

Try to include a few items in every outfit that are unusual, for example a white pair of shoes or a stylish hat. These sort of things normally attract attention from women and can give them good excuses to compliment you.

You should make an effort to improve your body language as much as possible. Most guys slouch too much, look down at the ground when they're walking and talk too fast (especially if they're nervous). Try to exhibit body language that reflects confidence and being comfortable with yourself. The most important things are to stand and walk with your shoulders held back, your chest out, and your chin up; to walk slowly with your eyes focused straight ahead (not looking at the ground and not looking around too much); and to sit with your back straight and your legs comfortable.

When you speak, articulate what you want to say clearly and at a reasonable pace. It's tempting if you're nervous to speed up or to add lot of unnecessary words. Try to avoid doing this. Don't be afraid to pause when you are stressing a point or waiting for input from the other person. As we've seen in the Approaching chapter, pausing can be very powerful.

Developing strong body language and speech consistently can take time. The easiest way to do it is to implement all the right body language and speech controls consciously for a period of a few weeks or a month. Eventually you will start to exhibit them unconsciously and be able to correct yourself when you slip up.

2. Confidence

Daytime approaching is a great way to demonstrate your confidence to women. Most guys with a few drinks inside them can muster the courage to approach a woman in a nightclub, but very few men who haven't read this book are able to do so in the glaring light of day.

A confident man is one who is willing to take risks for what he wants, is willing to lead and not just follow others, and is assertive when he needs to be. Women correlate confidence with success in life (for good reason), so become attracted to confident men.

Your appearance is going to give a woman an initial estimate of your confidence, but you should also try to get into conversation topics that further demonstrate you are a confident guy. For example, have you just moved to a new city? Do you do any particularly challenging activities in your spare time that indicate confidence, such as skydiving or mountain climbing? Are you starting your own business? These are good things to talk about because they show you're an inherently confident person.

Another important way to show confidence is simply to lead the interaction. If you progress things emotionally, physically and logistically without waiting for suggestions from her to do so, it'll show her that you're confident in yourself. So be the one to lead the conversation, be the one to ask her out and be the one to ask her to come back to your place. Don't wait for her to suggest or take charge of these things.

3. Humor

In the daytime, making a woman you just met laugh instantly relaxes the interaction and transforms it from "two strangers having a potentially awkward conversation" to "two people who just met having fun." It is not absolutely fundamental that this happens within the first few minutes, but it can help a lot.

Be light-hearted, don't take yourself or the situation too seriously, and don't be afraid to have fun with her. As said earlier, you shouldn't engage in heavy disqualification, but a little teasing is fine.

If the situation is awkward (for example, her mother turns up after you have approached her), a good sense of humor about the situation can help to diffuse it: "Oh my god, I had no idea I'd be meeting your mother so soon!"

Humor can also be useful if you are trying to progress the interaction and she is hesitant. For example, if she is reluctant to give you her phone number, you can tease her with:

Really? How I am I going to call you twenty times a day then? Damn it. I was planning to go home, sit by my phone and spend four hours composing the perfect text message. Now that plan is out of the window, I really don't know what I am going to do with the rest of my afternoon.

4. Social Intelligence

Social intelligence means having an understanding of social situations and how to deal with them appropriately. Generally speaking the more socially intelligent someone is, the more friends they will have and the more they will be able to get along with strangers and new people. Women know that men with social intelligence tend to be more successful in life.

Part of social intelligence is knowing that you are going to treat her respectfully and treat her well, and part of it is knowing that you will be able to function well in her world. For example, if you demonstrate a lack of social intelligence by ignoring her friends, she will naturally expect that you would make a bad impression on her family if she was ever to introduce you to them. The little things you do early on in an interaction can thus be indicators of how you will be in a relationship with her.

Look for cues in the situation to adjust how and when you talk to her. For example, if she's busy, show that you understand that by keeping your conversation brief, explaining that she intrigues you and you'd like to talk more another time.

If she's with friends, make sure to pay some attention to them and involve them in the conversation. If you have a friend or wingman (a friend who is there to meet women with you), you can get him to talk to the friend of the woman you're interested in.

If she's at work and you'd like to approach her, make sure that she isn't busy with customers and that her manager isn't hovering around keeping an eye on her.

"Cold reading", the practice of making inferences about someone based on subtle cues from them, is another great way of showing social intelligence. A lot of cold reading is about truisms, but you can also do more inspired "warm reads" when you have gotten to know a lot of people and can infer character traits more accurately.

For example, if a woman looks shy, you could say, "You know, you seem like the kind of person who can be really shy sometimes, but I bet when there is something you really want, you are willing to take risks for it." Or if a woman looks very stylishly dressed, you could say, "You seem like the kind of person who takes pride in her appearance. I like that. First impressions are so important."

You can also use cold reading to transition across conversation topics, for example, "You carry yourself really well. I'm guessing that you're a dancer or you've done some dancing in the past?" or "You look like you're a student. Do you study at UCLA?"

5. Passion

Passion is one of the most underrated sources of attraction for women. Women love a man who is passionate about things in his life. It could be his work, his hobbies, his family, friends or something else.

They like to see drive in men and they like to see evidence of that drive. It's not enough to just be interested in something; you should show that you are acting on that interest. For example, if you say you're passionate about music, do you go to a lot of concerts or play an instrument yourself? If you're passionate about your job, are you putting in extra hours at the office and doing a bit of work on the weekends?

Let women know subtly that you are acting on your passions through the topics of conversation you bring up, the emotion you express about them, and the concrete actions you are taking in that area.

Ideally, you want to see if you can find a few common passions between you and the woman you approach. The more she's interested in whatever it is you're passionate about, the greater the attraction building effect will be. You can often relate distinct passions by themes. For example, if she's into yoga, you can relate that to sports or martial arts, which you may be interested in.

6. Pre-selection

Pre-selection is when you are favored by other women already. A beautiful woman has so many men chasing her that it can be frustrating to give all of them enough attention to filter the attractive ones from the time wasters. Going on the recommendations of other women who have a similar or higher level of social value to them, whether those recommendations come explicitly or implicitly, can be a useful shortcut.

A woman will infer a certain amount of pre-selection from how you carry yourself (for example, a good level of confidence suggests that you have at least some experience with women). She'll also listen to how you talk about your life and the things you do. Do you have female friends that you hang out with? Do you have friends that come over to cook for you sometimes (if a "friend" is coming over to cook for you, she'll likely infer that that friend is female)?

Pre-selection doesn't have to mean that you are sleeping with lots of women, just that other women find you attractive. Don't try too hard to show her that you've been with a lot of women or that you have lots of female friends interested in you. Too much pre-selection can backfire (though you can often balance it out if you build stronger Qualification), so be careful.

7. Status

Having high status means having authority and power, which women like both for evolutionary reasons (men with these attributes tend to have better genes) and for social reasons (it can lead to a more interesting dating experience for women).

Status is relative depending on context. For example, a university professor has high status in his classroom, but on the football field the quarterback has more status than him. You can also indirectly get status benefits by being around or associated with people of high status, which is why men in the entourage of famous people often get a lot of attention from women.

Having a strong social circle with people around you that respect you is a good sign of status. Knowing a lot of people in other social circles can be useful too. A lot of times, when I can't think of a better way to relate to something a woman says, I will end up saying, "I have a few friends that do that."

If you have any positions of real power (for example, you are a public speaker or you are captain of a sports team), leverage them by subtly drawing the conversation towards topics where your positions might come up.

8. Wealth

Wealth is attractive to women for similar evolutionary and social reasons that status is. Most women want a man that has some degree of financial comfort, typically one equal to or greater than hers.

If you have a lot of wealth, be careful how you display it. Be subtle and only let on to your wealth slowly. It's also better for her to see it rather than for you to tell her about it; for example, her coming back to your place and seeing that it's clearly an expensive place is better than telling her, "I have a luxury condo in Beverly Hills."

If you don't have much money, it's not a big deal. Just make sure you don't look like you're struggling. Don't bring up any financial worries and don't make an issue of expenses. Also, demonstrate some ambition and potential to have greater wealth later in life. Men who are on their way up in the world are very attractive to women.

Accumulating Life Experience

For a long time when I was younger and would try to meet women, I would see them hooking up with older guys and wonder why. Since finding Love Systems, I've gradually broken down what I was doing wrong and what these guys were doing right.

One factor that directly affects the Attraction values we are able to demonstrate to a woman is life experience. The more we have done in our lives and the more real world knowledge we have, the more attractive we are to women.

For example, traveling experience relates to confidence (adventurousness); cultural experience relates to social intelligence; and business experience relates to status. If a particular experience does not relate to any Attraction Switches, then it is probably not worth discussing in conversation with a woman.

Some types of experience are more attractive to certain women than others. Having the skill to milk a cow for example, is probably not as attractive to most women as having the skill to salsa dance – unless of course, cow milking is useful to her or valuable in her society; for example, in a farming community.

Do not despair if you are young. At the time of writing this, I am twenty-six years old. I know guys my age or younger who have more life experience than me, and guys that are decades older with less. Although experience is roughly proportional to age, what really determines it is how you approach life. Do as much as you can do, try as many new things as you can, read, listen, learn and observe everything you can or wish to and you will gain more life experience than most.

You have had a certain amount of experience in your life so far. Search your memory for cool things you have done and think about how they relate to where you are now and when they might be relevant in a conversation. For example, if you are talking to a woman from Paris, think have you a) been to Paris yourself before, b) had a girlfriend from Paris, c) had a friend who lived in Paris, d) read about it and always wanted to go, or e) heard good things about it. These are all ways to relate to what a woman is saying and demonstrate some level of experience in your life (Chapter 17 of Magic Bullets has some great tips on storytelling that will help your ability to do this).

If you are an older gentleman, then you should have a lot of life experience under your belt. This should give you a lot to talk about – but remember, make sure it all relates back to the Attraction values. If you haven't got a lot of life experience behind you, you need to ask yourself the honest question, "Should I be doing more?" I will tell you now that it is never too late. I've seen older guys do amazing things after they've realized how they truly want to live their lives – from meeting young, beautiful women in the daytime to travelling the world in search of cultural and personal inspiration.

A great example of someone with a massive amount of accumulated life experience is my good friend Starlight. He has worked in the investment banking, SEO, green energy and corporate technology industries; he travelled through Europe as a teenager, toured the USA as a famous rock star and has visited many countries to teach Love Systems programs . All of these things allow him to relate to and demonstrate value to a diverse range of women.

A great book to read if you feel like you haven't done enough in your life is Yes Man by Danny Wallace. The hero of the story realizes one day how boring his life is and decides to say "Yes" to every opportunity that presents itself to him for a year. It's an inspirational story and I think we can all learn from it.

How to show your value

So now you understand the main sources of value that can generate Attraction, let's look in more detail at the four major ways you can demonstrate your value to a woman.

Live demonstrations are when a woman sees your value first-hand. It could be that she sees you making conversation with other strangers (demonstration of Social Intelligence), that you ask her to have a cup of coffee with you (demonstration of Confidence) or that she comes back to your place and sees one of your golfing trophies (demonstration of Passion).

Showing a woman a live demonstration is the most powerful way demonstrating value. Imagine the richest man in the world telling you he is the richest man in the world. You would be more impressed if you could see some first-hand evidence of his wealth; for example, a mansion or a private island.

Authority demonstrations are when a woman sees that you understand a topic and have experience within it, without you directly telling her why. In other words, you show that you have knowledge on a topic, but you don't mention the details of how you came to acquire that knowledge.

For example, if you visited Japan for a few months to train in Kendo (Japanese sword fighting), you could show a bit of value by telling a woman, "I went to Japan last year for three months and trained in the art of Kendo with some of the top samurai in the country." This is anecdotal evidence, as we'll come onto below.

But if you omit the anecdotal details and instead show authority of the subject of Japan or Kendo, then it will show even more value. For example, if you're in a Japanese restaurant, you could say, "I love watching Japanese chefs make sushi. The Japanese have an attention to detail and a work ethic unparalled by most other cultures in the world. It's just like how they practice Kendo. Even though it can be a violent sport, there's a beauty and a grace in how the two opponents move in relation to each other."

This isn't about trying to "one-up" someone with knowledge. When you do an authoritative demonstration of your value, show that you understand the area the other person is talking about and offer value to the conversation by sharing interesting or useful information on it.

When you are showing a woman your value, authoritative demonstrations are the most powerful method you have after live demonstrations.

Anecdotal demonstrations are when you tell a woman a story or something about yourself that directly implicates your value. The obvious way to do this is in the form of simple identity or achievement statements, for example, "I'm a musician," or "I go rock climbing at the weekends." The more subtle and more powerful way to do it is to embed it in the context of something else, for example, "Rome is really interesting, I was on tour there last year," or "Can you grab that for me? I hurt my arm when I was climbing last weekend."

Third-party demonstrations come from other people telling the woman about your value, for example, a friend of yours or a stranger mentions to her that you are a musician or that you are a national rock-climbing champion. This is an enormously powerful source of evidence – because it comes from a source less biased than you – but oftentimes is out of your control. The major thing you can do to facilitate third party evidence for your value is bring the women you meet into your social circle or to a venue where you have good relationships with people there. They will talk positively about you and that will make the woman more attracted to you.

Let's look at some examples of statements you could make that would show value. Have a think about what kinds of value you think they show.

> *The food in Rome is incredible; Italian food everywhere else doesn't taste quite as good as it does there.*
>
> *Most people are afraid of taking risks for the things they want in life. When I approached you, I had no idea what you were going to say or be like, but I'd*

rather find out than not. It's the same with starting a new business.

I think it's important to be open-minded in life. I know that in the music world, if you shut yourself off to new musical perspectives, you end up producing the same tune over and over again. But by being experimental and looking at other perspectives, you gain new inspiration. It's the same with meeting new people.

Now let's have a look at how attraction statements can be worked into an initial conversation.

John: *Excuse me, I just saw you walking towards me and I had to tell you that you look incredible. This outfit is so elegant and the way you walk is so graceful.*

Sarah: *Thank you!*

John: *What's your name?*

Sarah: *Sarah.*

John: *I'm John, pleased to meet you, Sarah. So what are you doing today?*

Sarah: *Oh I'm just going to meet some friends for lunch.*

John: *That's cool. I was actually just going to meet some friends when I saw you walking past. They are going to be annoyed with me for being late by talking to you, but I know I would be more annoyed if I let you walk past without saying hello. So tell me Sarah, what do you do for a living?*

Sarah: *I'm an accountant.*

John: *Yes, I thought so. You have a very "calculated" way of walking. I didn't know accountants were allowed to be this attractive. I figured you had to be a geeky dude with glasses. The guys in the office must go nuts over you. What made you get into accounting?*

> **Sarah:** *Well, the pay is good and the work isn't too hard. It's a pretty good deal overall.*
>
> **John:** *I can understand that. A lot of my friends in the city went into the field. I thought about it for a while, but I found numbers weren't my thing. I like business, but I wanted to throw some creativity into it, so I ended up going into marketing.*

Notice how John is making statements after every answer instead of firing a question straight back. In these statements he demonstrates some kind of value, whether it's humor, confidence, passion, status etc. and then asks another question to allow Sarah to open up further.

Signs of attraction

As you build attraction with a woman you're talking to, you want to be able to read whether she is getting attracted to you or not. The more attracted she is to you, the more likely you can engage in further Emotional, Physical and Logistical Progression.

In the context of a short daytime approach and conversation, the main things you are looking to do is Emotionally Progress into Qualification, and Logistically Progress into securing and organizing a date with her. The more signs of attraction you see as you converse with her, the more likely you'll be able to proceed into these stages.

Different women do different things when they are attracted to a man, but the below list shows some of the more common signs of attraction you should look out for in the daytime:

- She reinitiates conversation when you stop talking.

- She giggles.

- She plays with / tosses her hair.

- She asks you for your name or any other personal questions (e.g., age, where you live).

- She compliments you on anything.

- She is laughing, smiling, and/or holding eye contact with you.

- Both her feet are pointing towards you. If you stopped her on the street, both feet pointing towards you generally indicate she is engaged in what you're saying and not thinking about leaving.

- She doesn't make excuses to leave. This is especially relevant for a woman you stop on the street as she's walking. If she doesn't make an excuse to go within a minute or two, she is most likely attracted.

However, don't get too hung up on waiting for all or even some of these signals before trying to progress the interaction. For one, it's a man's responsibility to progress romantic and sexual interactions, and a woman's responsibility to exert a choice whether she wants to go along with it or not.

Too many guys wait for some kind of a "green light" from a woman before they ask her out, try to kiss her, or otherwise try to move the interaction forward. At higher stages of dating skill, this does indeed demonstrate high social intelligence. However, without a lot of practical experience of recognizing and acting on the above signals, most men tend to "play it safe" and end up not progressing things with women, when those women actually wanted them to – but perhaps weren't as confident in expressing to the man that they wanted to go further.

So as you are practicing your dating skill, don't look for a green light as much as you look for the absence of a red light. The ultimate litmus test of Attraction is trying to progress the interaction and seeing whether she goes along with it.

For two, no sign is definitive. A woman can do some of the things on this list without being attracted to you, or she can engage in none of them and still be attracted. These are guides, not laws of physics. It is easy to get addicted to signs of attraction. They feel good, and if you're not used to them, they feel like little wins ("This beautiful woman is actually attracted to me!"). However, inducing too many of these signs without moving on to Qualification is counterproductive, and gets boring for women. The end goal of a sexual relationship is more exciting than these signs anyway.

Chapter Summary

- Attraction is based on showing women that you have high social value.

- In the daytime, your Attraction phase will likely be shorter than it is at night, you don't need to do as much Disqualification, and you should focus more on demonstrating Passion than being Challenging.

- You should focus on demonstrating an attractive "snapshot" of yourself within the initial five-minute conversation using the different attraction switches.

- The 8 different attraction switches you can use to build social value are Appearance, Confidence, Humor, Social Intellgence, Passion, Pre-selection, Status and Wealth.

- You can leverage these attraction switches by using live demonstrations, authority demonstrations, anecdotal demonstrations, or third-party demonstrations. In initial daytime conversations, you will tend to use authority and anecdotal demonstrations the most.

- Good signs that you are building Attraction with a woman are when she engages in the conversation, she giggles or laughs, she touches herself (e.g. her hair or her arm) while she talks to you, both feet are pointing towards you, and she doesn't make excuses to go.

Chapter 8: Qualification

What is qualification?

Once a woman has become attracted to you, she wants to know that you're attracted to her for reasons other than just physical ones. We call this process Qualification.

It's still a good idea to express physical interest in a woman (and as we've seen in Approaching, it can a great way to start a conversation in the daytime), but this needs to be combined with compliments on her personality and achievements as well.

Qualification consists of screening and rewarding. Screening is where you assess whether a woman meets your standards and rewarding is where you show her that she meets your standards (if indeed, she does) – mostly by complimenting her.

Qualification is important because:

- High quality men have high standards for women in their life. By showing a woman that she meets specific standards you have set, she will be more attracted to you.

- Showing women your appreciation for who they are makes them more inclined to spend time with you. She may be attracted to you, but if she feels like she's just going to be another notch on your bedpost, she is less likely to act on it because there could be negative biological or social consequences for her; for example, getting pregnant or having other people think of her as a slut.

If you don't qualify a woman after building Attraction with her, it will be hard to progress the interaction physically and logistically. You can sleep with some women without much qualification, particularly younger girls or girls that party a lot. But in most cases, without expressing anything other than physical interest in a woman, you will struggle to get her to come home with you.

You should begin Qualification once a woman is attracted to you (see for more details on how to recognize when this is). Once a woman knows that you are attracted to her, the Qualification phase is complete. However, bear in mind that you will need to maintain Qualification levels when you are in Comfort (see Love Systems Triad).

Qualification in daytime dating

There are two major differences in Qualification for daytime dating compared with meeting women in nighttime venues.

- *Qualification often happens a lot sooner in the daytime than it does in bars and nightclubs.*

Because Attraction tends to be built in the daytime a lot quicker than it is in bars and nightclubs, you can move into the Qualification phase sooner. As you become more experienced with building Attraction, you may find that you move into Qualification very quickly – sometimes you can even do so immediately after Approaching if you feel that the woman is already attracted to you.

- *Qualification often runs a lot deeper in the daytime than it does in bars and nightclubs.*

Women in bars and clubs tend to be drinking, distracted by their friends and have multiple guys competing for their attention. These issues are mostly absent in the daytime, so you can get into real and direct conversations with women much more easily. This allows you to discover a lot of genuine things you like about a woman beyond her looks. Of course, it also runs the other way: if a woman isn't interesting beyond her looks, it will become apparent to you very quickly.

Screening

In order to find out if a woman meets your standards, you need to decide what those standards are in the first place. What kind of women do you want in your life? Do you like women who are adventurous, ambitious, sociable or feisty for example?

Write down a list of five things that are important to you in a woman's personality. Then, next to each one, write down a few examples of what a woman might have going on in her life that would reflect that quality. For example, I really like a woman to be very open-minded, which could be reflected by her traveling a lot, having a really varied taste in music, or being willing to try new things regularly.

Screen women you meet by introducing these specific topics into the conversation. Do so gently; you don't want to sound like you are interviewing her, rather that you are politely feeling her out to see whether she matches what you're looking for in a woman.

Topics that typically allow you find out a lot about a woman's personality include:

- Career

- Education

- Travel

- Hobbies

- Music and movies

- Fitness and sporting activities

- Social activities

Let's say I decided that I wanted a woman who was very sociable and had a lot of friends. I could screen for that by finding out about her social activities:

> **Jeremy:** *So tell me, do you go out a lot?*
>
> **Julia:** *Hmmm yeah! Quite a bit.*
>
> **Jeremy:** *Ah, so you're a party girl. I like that. What sort of places do you normally go to?*
>
> **Julia:** *Well, I'm not really into clubbing. I used to go to nightclubs all the time, but I prefer going to lounge bars these days.*
>
> **Jeremy:** *I'm the same. I enjoy good conversation with good people. You can do that in a lounge bar, but try doing it in a nightclub and you end up with a hoarse voice the next day. You know, you have a kind of dangerous look in your eyes – are you the kind of girl who tries to get all your friends drunk??*
>
> **Julia:** *Oh no! Not me. I'm very well behaved.*
>
> **Jeremy:** *Yes. Either that, or you're very good at pretending that you are [said with a smile so she knows I'm teasing].*

Notice that I start with a very general screening question and then get more specific as I get more positive input from the woman. Also, I'm using statements in between questions to keep Attraction levels up and to ensure she doesn't feel like she's being interviewed.

Some final notes on screening:

- Screen for things that you genuinely want in a woman. Daytime dating gives you a chance to have honest conversations with women really easily. Take advantage of that by having a serious think about the kind of women you like and figuring out what sort of questions you could ask to find them.

- It's really important to relate back to her answers with your own opinions and experiences in between asking her questions. Most guys ask women way too many questions early on without contributing any material to the conversation themselves – don't be one of those guys!

- Screening is one of the most useful tools you have if you find yourself running out of things to say when you are talking to a woman: if you lead the conversation onto a topic that interests you, you will probably have a lot you can say on it.

What If She Doesn't Meet Your Standards?

If you screen a woman on something and she doesn't match up to what you want, don't give up straight away. Change the topic and see whether she meets any of your other standards. No one is going to match up 100% to everything you want, so be willing to have some flexibility (besides, what you think you want won't necessarily be what you end up enjoying the most).

However, it's worth having some threshold minimum criteria that women absolutely need to meet. For example, my "deal breakers" are:

- She does nothing interesting in her spare time beyond partying

- She doesn't travel and expresses no interest in doing so

- She disrespects my friends

If a woman doesn't meet your minimum standards, politely excuse yourself and walk away. There are many, many more women out there to approach that just might have what you're looking for.

Compliments

The main way to reward women for meeting your standards is to compliment them. You should weave a few light but sincere compliments into the conversation early on, as soon as a woman starts responding positively to your screening topics.

Here are some examples:

- You're actually really cool to talk to.

- I think that's really attractive in a woman.

- I like that you carry yourself so well.

- I think it's great you're so ambitious.

- You seem like a really open-minded person. I like that.

Compliments shouldn't be overused. If you compliment a woman too often, she won't feel like she's earned them. Space them out with plenty of conversation in between. Also, don't always deliver compliments straight after seeing a quality you like; sometimes it's good to wait until later to tell her. The slight unpredictability means she'll be more excited about you praising her when you do.

As you get to know a woman better, you can compliment her more deeply. To do this, be more specific with your compliment. For example, "I like how confident you are" is a light compliment. After spending more time with her, you could say, "I like how confident you are. You take risks with things where other people would be too afraid. It's really rare to find someone with that kind of bold attitude to life."

After you deliver a compliment to a woman, don't let it linger or wait for a response. You don't want there to be a pause as if you expect her to suddenly express her undying gratitude for what you just said. Throw the compliment out and then move straight onto the next topic of conversation.

Here are some other guidelines for compliments:

- Compliments should be genuine. Don't pretend like you love everything about the woman you just met. Instead, look for her positive qualities and reward her for those.

- Try to compliment her on things that aren't immediately obvious. The less often she hears it from people, the more powerful it will be.

- Physical compliments are ok so long as they are used in moderation and you don't dwell on them. They're much better if they involve some element she has control over, for example her hair, the way she carries herself or her style (as opposed to her eye colour or her skin tone).

You should aim to give a woman a few compliments (around two or three) within the initial conversation you have with her when you meet her. By giving her explicit compliments on her personality (and not just her physical self), you're emphasizing to her that the two of you are a good match. It also communicates that you didn't just stop her to be friendly, but you actually have some romantic interest in her. That way, if she stays in the conversation, she is giving her implicit consent for you to pick her up – and therefore she's much more liable to agree to a date when you ask her out at the end of the conversation (which we'll cover in Logical Progression).

Let's look at an example of doing some screening and then weaving a compliment into the conversation.

> **Jeremy:** *You give off a creative vibe. Tell me, do you do something creative for a living or in your spare time?*

Julia: *Well... I work in advertising, but I do painting in my spare time.*

Jeremy: *That's great. I'm pretty analytical myself, so I find I'm always drawn to people more on the creative side. Thinking about it, when I first saw, I figured you'd be that sort of person. The way you're dressed and the way you walked was so expressive – I guess your energy spills over into your body language. I find that attractive.*

Julia: *Thanks [blushes].*

Chapter summary

- Qualification means appreciating a woman for her non-physical qualities, i.e. her personality.

- It's important to build Qualification so that a woman feels more comfortable taking an interaction further with you. If you don't make her feel appreciated, she won't feel comfortable going to bed with you.

- Qualification is based on screening for the personality characteristics you like, and then giving her compliments based on those.

- If she doesn't meet your standards, you should walk away or otherwise end the conversation politely.

- You should aim to throw a few compliments into your initial five-minute conversation with her so that she gets the sense that you are romantically interested in her, and not just chatting to be social. This makes her more likely to agree to go out with you when you do ask her out.

Chapter 9: Conversation Mapping

What is conversation mapping?

Now that you understand how Attraction and Qualification work, let's take a look at how to put all of this into a five-minute conversation. To do this, you can use a technique I designed called Conversation Mapping, which applies a simple but powerful structure that allows you to build Attraction and Qualification very quickly and efficiently.

You can actually use Conversation Mapping for any situation where you might meet a woman, though there will probably be some adjustments depending on the situation. As an example of an adjustment that might be made for a different situation, we'll see that "work" is one of the fields of the Conversation Map. However, in a nightclub, work isn't necessarily a good topic to bring up early on (instead it's often better to stay on more fun or humorous topics and possibly get into work later).

The beauty of Conversation Mapping is that it gives you a guide to talk a perfect stranger and have a good shot at establishing a connection with them within just a few minutes. Many of my clients have said to me, "I just don't know what to say when I first meet a woman!" This technique gives you a game plan for just that.

In a way, it's almost like a game of chess when you first meet a woman. You can't just move a piece without thinking: you have to be wondering what the possible consequences of moving that piece could be. In other words, you have to be thinking several steps ahead.

It's the same in Conversation Mapping. When you ask a question about what she's up to or her work or something else, you're not just asking the question idly (which is what most guys do simply to prolong the interaction and "keep" her there). No. You have a specific plan with specific conversational routes you are trying to go down.

Have a quick look over the following diagram to get an overview of Conversation Mapping, and then we'll go through each aspect of it in detail.

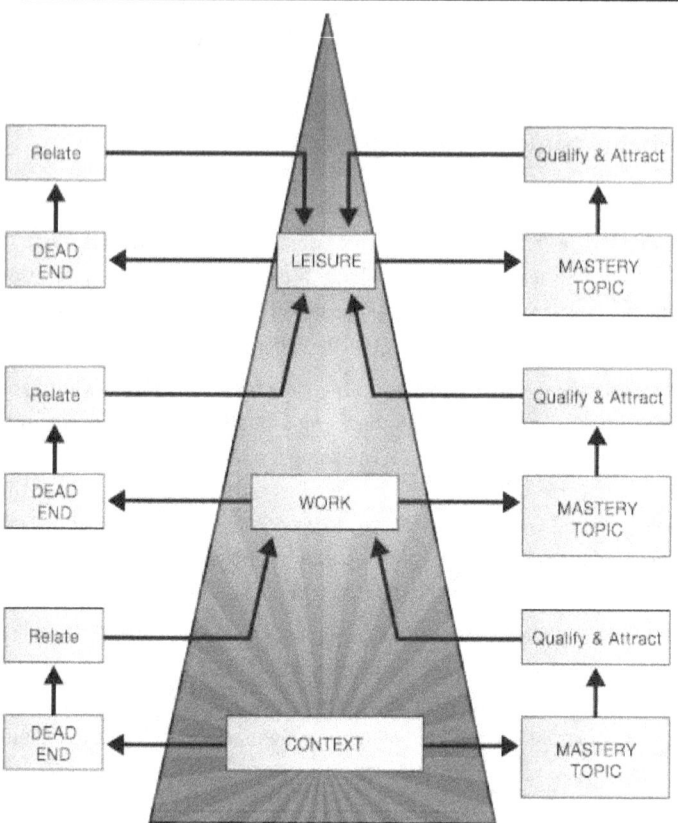

Context, work & leisure

Through many thousands of approaches, I realized that there were three fields of conversation that I normally went through when I met a woman: context, work and leisure.

Context is about discussing the current situation you meet her in. In the daytime, it normally starts with you seeing her walking past, sitting down, or standing somewhere and wanting to come talk to her (as you explain when you approach her). After the approach, there's still a bit more context to establish. For example, what is she doing when you meet her? Is she on her way somewhere, is she studying in a café, or is she a tourist in town wandering around trying to find things to do?

Context will sometimes allow you to get onto interesting things. For example, maybe she's an aspiring actress and on her way to a casting which she's excited about. On the other hand, it could be something more mundane, like she's out shopping for groceries. Whether or not you manage to land on something interesting (and by "interesting," I mean interesting to the both of you), establishing the context is a good way of breaking the social ice and easing her into a more comfortable conversation.

Context can also involve where she's from or you're from, especially if it's clear that she's relatively new to town or only travelling through (or indeed, you are). It's a less interesting topic if it's clear you're both from that place and have lived there a long time. (This reflects a general conversational principle whereby things that are newer to us are more emotionally relevant and often more interesting to talk about.)

A typical context question is something like, "So what are you doing today?" As we'll see shortly, asking that question itself doesn't really generate any Attraction, but allows you to guide the conversation towards things that could be potentially interesting. As a rule-of-thumb, never ask a question without knowing where you're going with it. Within the first few minutes, you should always be planning to reach specific topics where you have interesting or funny things to say. At the very least, know your answer to every question you ask her. For example, in the case of context, be prepared to tell her what you're up to today (and make sure it shows some social value) if you're asking her the same.

Once you've established some context and broken the ice a little, the second field is work. Some people wonder if work is a good topic to bring up. It may be, it may not be, depending on whether you each enjoy your jobs. Regardless, it certainly forms most of our daily lives as human beings, so by finding out about work we can find out a lot about each other. So you can ask her what she does for a living, perhaps going on to say what you do for a living.

The key is not so much about finding out random facts about her, but rather finding out how your lives relate to each other, and how you can demonstrate social value to this particular woman based on the aspects of her life. We'll cover this shortly when we talk about Mastery Topics, but as an example, if you find out that she's training to be a lawyer, and you're already a lawyer with a prestigious law firm, then suddenly you have a good opportunity to build social value and thus attraction.

You may not get these opportunities in the work field of conversation, so the third and final field is leisure: what you both do in your spare time for fun. Asking a woman, "What do you do for fun?" often leaves her a bit unsure what to say, so try to lead her down possible routes by asking if she's interested in specific things. For example, from "What do you do for fun?" you could add, "I mean, are you a party animal, do you like to go out a lot, or are you more the stay-at-home-and-read type?" You could even try something as simple as, "Are you into travelling, sports... music?"

In general, it's important to cover all three fields (context, work and leisure) in your initial conversation. Moreover, that specific order will help the flow of conversation because each field is progressively more intimate. If you were to start with the leisure question, you might find that a woman doesn't open up easily. But if you've gone through context and work, and hopefully built some Attraction within those fields, then you'll be able to move onto leisure much more easily.

Remember, as discussed in the Attraction chapter when we talked about Snapshot Theory, you don't want to focus on any one topic or attraction switch as your sole source of social value, but cover a wide range of topics. Going through these three fields helps facilitate that.

And just to reiterate, remember that asking about context, work or leisure isn't by itself attractive, but rather it gives you a roadmap to get onto things that are more interesting. Everyone is interested in talking about different things. Some people love their job, some people love sports, some people love travelling. Asking about context, work and leisure are simply avenues that will help you discover who she is, what she enjoys and what you can show social value on.

>   **Jeremy:** *So what are you doing today?*
>   **Jessica:** *I'm going shopping.*

Jeremy: *Cool. It's a great day to be out and about. I'm trying to work off a huge hangover from last night, so it's nice to be out in the sun! Tell me, what do you do for a living? Hmmm I'm guessing you do something creative from the way you're dressed?*

Jessica: *Well, yes, sort of. I work in advertising.*

Jeremy: *Oh, nice. I have a background in advertising myself... [Jeremy then builds Attraction and Qualification, using the advertising topic be cause he knows a lot about it. A few minutes later, he moves into the next field of conversation, leisure.]*

Jeremy: *I think it's great that you have such a cool job, but tell me, what do you do when you're not working? Are you a party animal, or more the stay-at-home-and-read type for example?*

Jessica: *Haha, yeah, I like to party....!*

Mastery topics

There are certain topics of conversation that as an individual you will feel very comfortable with. Possibly because you are passionate about that topic, you have a lot of experience in it, you have achieved a lot in that area or because you are ambitious about getting more into it. These topics are your Mastery Topics, and can be used to build Attraction and Qualification.

Some simple examples of Mastery Topics could be sports, the nightclub scene, travelling, advertising, or technology.

Importantly, a Mastery Topic should involve as many attraction switches as possible. For example, if you're good with computers, it doesn't necessarily mean that talking about why a certain type of programming language is better than another is a good idea. (Although if she happens to be interested in that, it might actually help; but it'd be rare to find a woman who is.) However, using "technology" as your Mastery Topic, and talking about how fast the world is evolving technologically and the impact it's having on our lives demonstrates Social Intelligence, Passion and possibly even Status if you are good in your field.

Talking about a Mastery Topic is like playing on home rather than away ground in sports: you know the arena, you know the variables, you have the advantage. The initial conversation you have with a woman in the first few minutes is so important that you should try to stay on home territory as much as possible, so you can demonstrate your social value.

Imagine for example, that you meet a woman and get into a conversation about something you know nothing about, like art. If she is knowledgeable about art and you're not, that topic is not going to allow you to show social value and therefore you probably won't build any Attraction (which you need to do as soon as possible) by staying on that topic. On the other hand, if she tells you her favourite art gallery is in France, and Europe is one of your Mastery Topics (because you spent a summer travelling there), then if you lead the conversation towards a discussion of Europe rather than art, you're on much better ground.

Mastery Topics are also only useful insofar as a woman is or could be interested in them. To continue the example, if Europe is one of your Mastery Topics, but she has never been to Europe, has no real interest in visiting it, and isn't interested in any of the culture there, then it probably won't be that useful to get onto Europe as a topic of conversation.

However, do try to think outside the box when it comes to relating Mastery Topics to things she might be interested in. For example, if you're an excellent and passionate golf player, then she might not be able to relate to golf or be interested in golf specifically, but she might have experienced the same sort of emotional feeling and stress release in yoga that you do with golf.

Finally, bear in mind that levels of Mastery in a topic are relative. If you're a professional writer, and she's an aspiring one, it's a good Mastery Topic to showcase your social value. On the other hand, if she's a professional writer and you're the aspiring one, it's not a bad topic to get onto, but not one you want to stay on for long in the early stages where you need to demonstrate your social value. When you get onto a topic where you don't have any Mastery or she has more Mastery than you, it's generally a good idea to relate to her a little, and then bridge out of it. We'll come onto Bridging and Relating shortly.

Building Attraction using Mastery Topics

Once you have led the conversation onto a Mastery Topic, you build Attraction on it by using "I-statements." An I-statement is a statement that uses the self to talk about something, for example: I did, I do, I know, I think, I feel, I want. The I-statements we want to use in Attraction should ultimately construct sentences that leverage the attraction switches.

For example, let's look at the following statement.

> *I love golf because it really helps me to de-stress from a long week of work. There's a course really close to me that's beautiful, and every Sunday my friends and I get together to debrief and play a few holes. No matter how stressed I am, I can always relax for those few hours on a Sunday.*

That's good for building attraction because it contains lots of I-statements which leverage attraction switches (working hard reflects Passion, having a golf course close by reflects Status, and getting together with friends every Sunday reflects Social Intelligence).

A bad set of things to say on the other hand, when bringing up golf would be:

> *Oh, you like golf? That's great! Where do you play? Oh I'm probably not as good as you. Have you played for a long time? You sound like you're a pro!"*

That's a bad set of things because it makes the interaction all about her, which in the beginning, when you're trying to build Attraction, it shouldn't be.

As a general rule, within the first five-minute conversation, you should be talking most of the time. About 70% of your conversation should be I-statements, and the rest should be questions that are used to guide and tailor the conversation.

Building Qualification using Mastery Topics

Mastery Topics are naturally good topics for Qualification. If these are the things that you are most interested and experienced in in life, then it's probably going to be hard to connect with a woman if she has no vestige of interest in those things.

She might not necessarily be directly interested in one of your Mastery Topics, but maybe she is interested in something related to or similar to it. For example, if you're into sports, she might not play anything herself but maybe she goes to the gym regularly, which comes under the banner of health and fitness. You can therefore demonstrate some social value and give compliments by leveraging the sports topic.

Note that Mastery Topics won't be the only things you qualify a woman on, but they're a good start. Once you've built a bit of Attraction with her using a couple of your Mastery Topics, you can ask more about her in relation to things you don't have Mastery over, to see if she could match what you're looking for. For example, law is not one my Mastery Topics, but I love finding out that a woman is a successful lawyer (because it often means she's intelligent, well-read, educated, articulate and ambitious). So although I don't use the law topic to build Attraction on, I do use it to give her a compliment or two.

Bridging

Bridging is how you get onto Mastery Topics (or how you end up at Dead Ends, which we'll come onto in a bit). Similar in nature to the Transitioning stage of the Love Systems Triad, there are two major types of bridges you can use.

The first is the **Logical Bridge**. This is where you search for a logical, factual connection between two topics. For example, asking a woman what she does for a living, what she does for fun, or whether she likes dancing are all Logical Bridges.

The second is the **Emotional Bridge**. This is where you search for an emotional connection between two topics. For example, asking a woman whether she enjoys her job, whether she does anything adventurous in her spare time, or what it is she enjoys about dancing. In these cases, you're trying to link topics by finding a similar feeling to her, even though what causes you each to have that feeling might be different.

You can use both questions and statements, separately or even together to make Logical and Emotional Bridges. Statements are generally more useful when you know you have to show a bit more social value in order to get her to open up (especially if she seems a bit hesitant to open up first of all).

Let's look at some examples.

> **Logical Bridge** (Question): *What do you do for a living?*
>
> **Logical Bridge** (Statement): *You look like... you're a lawyer. Smart, no-nonsense dress, upright posture, eyes that look like they could slay someone in a courtroom.*
>
> **Emotional Bridge** (Question): *Do you enjoy your job?*
>
> **Emotional Bridge** (Statement): *You look like someone who enjoys what she does. I think that's great. It's rare to meet people who actually are doing something they love.*

Dead ends

When you use Bridges, you're trying to manoeuvre the conversation onto your Mastery Topics. Occasionally, you'll hit Dead Ends, which are topics you know very little about (the opposite of Mastery Topics).

For example, when you ask a woman what she is doing and the response is "shopping," that could be a Dead End topic. To stay on it, for example, asking what she is buying or whether she shops a lot, could go nowhere fast. On the other hand, if you're interested in fashion (assuming she is out buying clothes), it could actually lead you onto a Mastery Topic.

But let's say it's a Dead End for you. You want to go onto something more interesting, but if you just shut down the conversation thread with an "Oh. Well what else do you do?" it's going to come across as socially awkward.

So instead, you want to relate to her just enough to grease the wheel of the conversation, and then Bridge out (hopefully onto something more interesting). If you can directly Bridge onto a Mastery Topic, great; if not, just move up the Conversation Map onto the next field of Conversation (i.e. progress from context to work or work to leisure).

Note that it will be difficult to have a good conversation if you haven't managed to get onto a single Mastery Topic by the time you've gone through the context, work and leisure fields. If that's happening a lot, it's probably Bridging that you need to work on.

Relating means to accept her statement in some way, perhaps saying what you can about it – your experience of that thing, relating the experiences your friends have had with it, or even just things you've heard about it.

For example, I don't know much about art, but if a woman brings up art in a conversation (maybe because I asked what she does for a living and she is an artist), I could say the following things to relate to her:

> *Oh that's cool. One of my friends is really into art and just bought a small gallery here [Relating]. Do you enjoy what you do [Bridging out]?*
>
> *Interesting. That makes a lot of sense – you seem like the creative type. I like that [Relating and a little Qualification]. So tell me, what do you do for fun, when you're not painting, I mean [Bridging out]?*
>
> *Nice. I never got into art much in school [Relating], but recently it dawned on me that I need to flex my creative muscles [Bridging out]. I'm in marketing so from time to time*

> *I need to brainstorm and think up new stuff. I find it quite challenging but at the same time, quite fun too.*

As said earlier, Mastery is relative. So if you realize a woman has more Mastery than you on a particular topic, consider relating to her just enough to show you have some social value on it, before you Bridge out.

Investment equilibrium

A lot of men make the mistake of trying too hard to impress women. I've seen this hundreds of times even with guys who claim they are "good with women." When you try too hard to prove your social value to people, it makes them feel like you are seeking their approval. Some guys fall into this trap by being overly cocky and funny in the first few minutes, instead of giving her a chance to talk and relating to her world a little.

Conversely, a lot of men make the opposite mistake of not trying hard enough to impress. They ask question after question, forgetting to talk about themselves and show the woman anything interesting about themselves. They try too hard to relate to her and are not proactive enough in demonstrating their social value.

You should try to achieve what I call an "Investment Equilibrium" in your conversations. This is when you lead the conversation down a good route, which then gets her to open up a little, allowing you to show some social value that is going to interest her, which then causes her to open up further and so on. In this way, you both invest gradually increasing amounts into the conversation to ensure that it's interesting for both of you, and that you are demonstrating the kind of social value she is interested in.

For example, if you like skydiving and ask her if she's interested in extreme sports, you need to check that she engages in that topic (possibly telling you that yes, she likes extreme sports, or maybe even just that yes, she's adventurous and wants to try skydiving sometime) before you launch into a skydiving story. If she is more of a bookworm type and doesn't bite on the extreme sports topic, then you'd be trying too hard to impress if you went into a long skydiving story.

When my friend and fellow Love Systems instructor, Mr. M, famously picked up a Playboy Playmate doing a daytime, he mentioned to her that he ran a club promotions company in London. That value was relevant to her because she was involved in the promotions industry. Had he mentioned it to a woman who worked as a painter and had no interest in socializing in nightclubs, it would have had a far lesser impact.

Getting good at Investment Equilibrium will take some time and a lot of practice. The line between showing you have enough value and trying too hard to impress can be a fine one. The easiest way to think about it is that when you ask a woman questions, you should generally make a few statements that show some relevant value before asking more questions, i.e. before asking her to invest more in the conversation.

- If you are only asking questions and not talking about yourself, you are probably not showing enough relevant value.

- If you are making lots of statements and she is barely saying anything, you are probably trying too hard to impress her.

Let's look at an example of not showing enough value.

> **Michael:** *You don't sound like you are from around here, where are you from?*
>
> **Katie:** *I'm from Canada.*
>
> **Michael:** *Canada? Cool! What are you doing here?*
>
> **Katie:** *Just on holiday.*
>
> **Michael:** *Cool! Do you like it?*
>
> **Katie:** *Yeah it's ok.*
>
> **Michael:** *Cool. What do you do for fun?*
>
> **Katie:** *Sorry, I really have to get going...*

In this dialogue, Michael didn't offer any relevant value or show that he had an opinion about things, a sense of humor, or any kind of relatable life experience. Katie has to excuse herself rather than explain herself to someone she doesn't see any value in.

Let's look at an example of trying too hard to show value.

> **Michael:** *You don't sound like you are from around here, where are you from?*
>
> **Katie:** *I'm from Canada.*
>
> **Michael:** *Oh cool. My ex-girlfriend is from Canada. I met her there while I was snowboarding last year and she was doing a photo shoot.*
>
> **Katie:** *Oh, cool.*
>
> **Michael:** *Yeah it was a fun for a while. I really love snowboarding – I'm training to enter the European championships this year.*
>
> **Katie:** *Oh, that's cool.*
>
> **Michael:** *Yeah it's a lot of hard work, especially because work is so busy right now – I'm a management consultant by the way. But to get anywhere in life takes sacrifice, you know? So listen, do you want to grab a drink with me some time?*
>
> ***Katie:*** *Oh thanks, but I have a boyfriend.*

In this dialogue, Michael tried too hard to show value and gave away lots of details about himself upfront without waiting to see whether Katie was interested in those details. When he asked her out, she made a polite excuse to duck out of it.

Finally, let's look at an example where Michael gets it right, demonstrating just enough relevant value to get Katie to open up and become attracted to him.

Michael: *You don't sound like you are from around here, where are you from?*

Katie: *I'm from Canada.*

Michael: *Awesome! I love Canadians – I find them to be the friendliest people on Earth. What are you doing in London?*

Katie: *Haha, yes we Canadians are cool! I'm just here for a holiday with friends.*

Michael: *Holiday, eh? I think you are just here to pick up cute English guys. What do you guys think of London so far?*

Katie: *Haha, maybe I am! It's really cool here, I like it. Everyone is so friendly and there's so much to do. It's much quieter where I'm from.*

Michael: *That's the cool thing about London. You can do almost anything you want here. And it's such a cosmopolitan city; you get to meet people from all over. So tell me Katie, what do you do for fun?*

Notice how Michael makes just enough value statements to reinforce the threads of discussion and lead the conversation towards topics of mutual interest – in this case, meeting people from different cultures and what it's like being in London.

Being able to structure and lead a conversation that demonstrates your social value with the right relevance and in the correct proportion is a skill that takes time to acquire. If you master it, doing so demonstrates social intelligence in itself.

Chapter summary

- Conversation Mapping is a method of building Attraction and Qualification very efficiently within a five-minute conversation with a woman.

- The three fields of the Conversation Map you should go through when you first meet a woman in the daytime are context (what is going on right now), work (what you and her do for work) and leisure (what you and her do for leisure).

- Using the Conversation Map, you should steer the conversation towards Mastery Topics, which are topics you are very knowledgeable about. Use these Mastery Topics to build Attraction (by making statements) and Qualification (by asking questions and giving compliments).

- You can Bridge between topics using logical or emotional links.

- Make sure you bear in mind how invested she is in a particular topic before you start talking about it a lot.

- If you get onto Dead End topics, Bridge out of them onto areas where you have Mastery.

Chapter 10: Comfort

What is comfort?

After building Attraction and Qualification with a woman, the next phase of Emotional Progression to consider is Comfort.

Comfort is the phase where you really "get to know" each other. This means opening up and sharing information about your lives with each other. For example, it includes sharing information about careers, hobbies, future goals, friends and family.

Most guys who aren't familiar with Magic Bullets and Love Systems methodology make the mistake of going into Comfort with a woman straight away, but don't forget that Attraction is the prerequisite of Comfort – if you don't show any social value to a woman, she has no reason to want to open up and share information about herself with you.

The Comfort phase is critical for making a woman feel comfortable enough to sleep with you. It shows a woman that you understand her, and are therefore more likely to be able make her feel good when she is with you. No matter how much Attraction or Qualification you build with a woman, in general you'll still need some level of Comfort to progress things.

In this chapter, we'll go over the key principles of sharing and empathizing that lie at the heart of Comfort, as well as the physical and logistical aspects of Comfort-building. First, let's take a look at how Comfort fits into daytime dating.

Comfort in daytime dating

Remember that the three parts of the Love System Triad – Emotional, Physical and Logistical Progression – should occur in sync. In the case of Comfort building, you need to be in a situation with a woman where you have ample time and are free enough of distractions to share things with each other. In daytime dating, this generally means setting up a date.

It might be a date that you suggest and set for a later time, or it might even be an instant date (where you go on a date with a woman after just a few minutes of meeting and talking with her). This is a key part of Logistical Progression and we'll cover it in detail in the next chapter. For now, realize that most of your Comfort building will take place on that date, and that your initial meeting and conversation with a woman should focus on Attraction and Qualification.

(Note that there's already some level of Comfort inherent to the process I outlined in Conversation Mapping, mainly because it involves talking about things you're passionate about – which as we'll see in this chapter, is important in the Comfort phase. However, the primary goal of Conversation Mapping is not Comfort, but rather to demonstrate your social value and recognize hers so that she might want to spend more time with you.)

When you get into Comfort (when you're on a date), your focus should shift into more emotional topics, sharing perspectives with her, and building a feeling of rapport. In that sense, Comfort is less about showing social value to her, and more about sharing emotional value with each other.

Remember also, that being in the Comfort phase doesn't mean you never need to do any Attraction or Qualification work ever again. Quite the contrary: you'll need to keep "topping up" Attraction and Qualification levels as you go through Comfort. You can't store emotions in the bank. So remember that her feelings will return to their prior state over time unless you keep up the Emotional Progression.

Comfort will form the bulk of your interactions with women after you've attracted and qualified them. You will probably spend a few hours building Comfort with a woman before you sleep with her. This may happen in one meeting, on the first date, or over the course of several meetings.

Ultimately, there are no hard and fast rules as to how long it takes to sleep with a woman. The main thing is to make sure you are progressing the interaction gradually as you spend more time with her. We'll cover Physical and Logistical Progression in detail in the next part of this book.

Sharing and empathizing

Sharing and empathizing are the foundations of Comfort. A woman wants to know that she can share details of her life and how she feels with you, and that you understand her. She also wants to see that you can do the same with her.

The more she shares with you, the more she'll feel comfortable with you. So it's in your interest to get her to open up. In other words, ask questions and find out more about her. Dig beyond the surface and really try to get to know her as a person: what are her passions, motivations, ambitions, desires, opinions and experiences in life?

Generally speaking, you'll build stronger Comfort if you focus on topics of emotional relevance to her. For example, if she has a strong feeling towards her job (whether it gives her a good or bad feeling), by sharing that with you, she'll feel more emotionally invested in you. On the other hand, if she isn't really bothered about her job, but gets excited more about what she does in her spare time, then her hobbies and interests are probably better topics to get into.

Here are some good topics for Comfort:

- Career and work

- Hobbies and Interests (for example, sports, travelling, music, movies, reading, art)

- Life goals and ambitions

- Friends and family

- Personal history (for example, where she grew up, early jobs, education)

As a woman shares information with you about these things, you should try to empathize with her and share your own related experiences. When you relate to a woman (or anyone, for that matter), you don't necessarily need to have experienced the same thing as them in logical terms to be able to empathize. Instead, it's more important to recognize the emotional content of what they're saying and empathize with that, sharing something that made you feel similarly.

For example, if a woman shares with you that she enjoys horse riding because she loves nature and it gives her a sense of freedom when she is riding, you don't necessarily have to have been horse riding yourself to relate to her. Maybe you experience a similar feeling when you ride your motorcycle or put the top down on your car on a sunny day, and could use that to relate to her experience.

If you cannot empathize with something – for example, you meet an accountant and you have nothing you think you can relate to on that field – then you can try to dig deeper into the topic or across to another topic to find something you can empathize with. To use the accountant as an example, here is how you could dig deeper into the topic of careers to find something you can relate to:

> **Amanda:** *I'm an accountant.*
>
> **Jeremy:** *Very cool. What do you enjoy about it?*
>
> **Amanda:** *Well, not much! It pays the bills...*
>
> **Jeremy:** *Haha, well tell me then, what would you dream job be?*
>
> **Amanda:** *Well... I've always wanted to be a singer.*
>
> **Jeremy:** *That's so cool. Imagine singing on a cruise ship and getting to travel the world. That would be amazing! Where would you travel to?*

Here is an example of digging across topics; in this case from careers to hobbies as a means to find something to relate to:

> **Amanda:** *I'm an accountant.*
>
> **Jeremy:** *Very cool. What do you do when you have time off?*
>
> **Amanda:** *Erm... I like hanging out with friends. Shopping, I guess.*
>
> **Jeremy:** *Sure, I love hanging out with friends too. But let me put it this way, if you had tomorrow off and I gave you $1m to do whatever you wanted to do, what would you do?*
>
> **Amanda:** *Haha... I think I would go on holiday. To Hawaii.*
>
> **Jeremy:** *That's awesome. I have a Hawaiian friend that is always telling me how beautiful it is there. I think I'll go visit her there and hang out someday.*

You don't always have to agree with everything a woman says or share her sentiment regarding an experience. I often have different views to the women I meet and spend time with. But I rarely invalidate their emotions by saying to them, "You're wrong." Instead, I say things like, "I see where you're coming from," or "That's an interesting perspective," and then state how I feel about it. In this way, although you may have different views on something, you can both empathize with each other on an emotional level.

As you spend more time with a woman, most likely on a date that you've set up after you've first met her, you should try to get to know her on a more personal level. This means getting into deeper emotional topics, for example finding out about her values and life ambitions. Here's an example of gradually getting a woman to open up more and more:

Here's an example of gradually getting a woman to open up more and more:

> John: *So tell me more about what you're going to do in Chicago. Will you be an accountant there also?*

Sarah: *I don't know exactly, yet. Maybe. Sometimes I'm not sure what I want to do.*

John: *I think a lot of people are that way at certain stages in their lives. It's almost like it's a continual process of trying to figure out what you really want, and stripping away all of the things that the world makes you think you want. What's important to you in life?*

Sarah: *My friends and my family I guess. I like doing new things, especially things with a lot of energy, like sports and dancing. I really love to cook, but I'm not sure whether I could be a chef.*

John: *Well, Chicago would be a great place to learn. They have some fantastic cuisine there. One of my best friends is a chef there and he always treats me to some amazing food. What do you feel is stopping you from being a chef?*

Sarah: *I'm not sure. I've been an accountant for so long. But it's boring, you know? The money is decent, but I'm just not passionate about it anymore. The thought of being a chef is so exciting!*

John: *Absolutely! I always love those kitchen challenge shows and think they're so much fun. It's amazing what they can with the most ridiculous ingredients. At the end of the day, learning any new profession takes hard work and a bit of time. Of course it's going to be strange trying to learn something new, but it sounds like you're going to be unhappy if you continue doing what you're doing now. On the other hand, it may feel strange learning a new trade, but you'll probably enjoy the process and be much happier within a few months time.*

Sarah: *I think you're right. I should just go do it. John, it's so easy to talk with you. I can't believe I just met you today in the park.*

John: *Well, I'm glad I came to talk to you. There are a lot of good-looking women in London, but it's rare to meet someone who's really passionate, intelligent and mature. I*

> think it's important to take chances to meet people that you might get along with. The same goes for your job: it might be a risk to try the whole chef thing, but it's better to try and find out than to always wonder what could have happened.

See how John asks Sarah questions to find out more about her, steering the conversation to good Comfort topics like life goals. He shares his own experiences, thoughts and feelings in return and then encourages Sarah to open up more.

Sarah feels comfortable in talking with John and gives him a nice compliment. He reciprocates and emphasizes why he likes her – giving her the feeling that she wouldn't just be another notch on his bedpost if she were to sleep with him.

Comfort Guidelines

As you get better at building Comfort, there are a few things you need to bear in mind.

- Keep the conversation as positive as possible. Don't talk negatively about your own life, and if she gets onto a topic that's negative for her, empathize but gently guide the conversation towards a more upbeat topic.

- Don't be cocky, disqualify, tease or make fun of her when she is opening up to you. Those things can be useful in the Attraction phase, but they can hamper things in Comfort (although if you sense Attraction levels are dropping, they might be useful in small doses to renew them).

- Don't be afraid to show a little vulnerability (so long as it is followed by positivity). For example, "I have a fear of heights and it makes me feel like a loser," is bad, but "I have an incredible fear of heights, so next year I've booked a skydiving trip so I can overcome it," is good.

- Don't be more emotional than her. You should try to guide her to open up to you, and then open up an equivalent amount yourself. If you start gushing about your feelings more than she does to you, it could be a real turn-off.

- More serious topics (and that often includes details of bad break-ups and past relationships) are best kept until later dates, possibly even once you've started dating more seriously. You don't want to be the shoulder a woman cries on until you've established a real relationship with her.

- Don't be judgmental about anything she says. Keep a completely open mind and be willing to learn from her as a person

- Talk in terms of the emotions behind things rather than the logical or material things themselves. For example, you don't establish more Comfort with a woman by telling her that you have a Ferrari. But you do by telling her that for a long time it was your dream to own a great sports car and that you had to work day and night for a long time to get to a point in your life where you could; and that now, you love nothing more than driving on an empty lane in the countryside as fast as you can because that's when you feel the most free.

Talking in Emotional Terms

Most men have a real issue with talking in terms of emotions, which is why they're never able to establish as deep a Comfort with women as they could. Women are naturally very in touch with their emotions, but as men, we push our emotions down and don't really understand how they affect us – and indeed, can empower us.

The trick to understanding and appreciating your emotions is to keep digging at the facts deeper and deeper until you get to the raw emotions that make certain experiences significant to you. Then when you are with a woman and want to tell her about one of these experiences, package up the emotions in a positive way and explain the events that led to these feelings.

Here's an example of something that actually happened to me while I was in Thailand. The facts of the experience are quite straightforward – I met a girl and had sex on the beach with her – but how I dress up the story is a great example of using emotive language in order to build Comfort. If you read it carefully, there is a lot of positive sentiment as well as frames of adventurousness, spontaneity, romance and sexuality. Don't repeat this to a woman yourself (because it didn't actually happen to you), but think about how you could use more emotive language to describe something that did happen to you.

Have you ever been to Thailand? It's incredible there. Honestly, I don't think I've ever felt as free in my entire life as I have when I was there.

I remember one night, I was travelling alone on one of the islands, Ko Pha Ngan. I had just left my friends on the last island, so I didn't know anyone there. I went to this huge Full Moon Party. There were people everywhere, drinking and dancing on the beach - it was crazy.

I chatted to a few people, but the crowd got too crazy for me, so I went for a walk. Towards the side of the beach I saw this absolutely beautiful girl sitting by herself. I don't think I've ever seen someone look so at peace with herself.

I asked her if I could join her and we started talking. About two hours later, we were both drunk on buckets of cocktails and staring out at the ocean. Something clicked between us, and between the alcohol, the sun setting and the soft, warm sand beneath us, it was like we were perfectly in sync with each other.

I'm not normally one for al fresco sex, but in that moment with her it was like everything else disappeared. It was just she and I in this beautiful little bubble, while the outside world partied and kept spinning without us.

I think sometimes it takes a feeling of freedom to be able to have a connection like that. Too often in the big city, people lose sight of that freedom. Do you know what I mean?

Physical comfort

Another strong component of Comfort, in addition to verbally sharing and empathizing with a woman, is how you are physically with her. That means your body language when you talk with her, how you look at her and how you touch her. Let's have a look at the main areas to be aware of.

Eye contact

Look her straight in the eyes when you listen to her. It sounds like a simple thing to do, but a lot of guys who aren't confident avoid it. If you can't look her in the eyes, then every other Comfort-builder you use will be wasted.

It's ok to look off into the distance, for example, slightly up towards a point in space, when you are telling a story or talking about something you are really passionate about (particularly in the Attraction phase). But for the majority of the time, and certainly whenever you are listening to her talk, you should maintain eye contact.

Smile

When you are telling her something that fills you with positive emotion, for example a story about how you travelled to Thailand, show her that by smiling. When you are listening to her, empathize with her good feelings by smiling.

However, be careful not to smile all the time she is talking; this looks like you are trying too hard to empathize (remember, a guy who over-empathizes doesn't build good Comfort). The best way is to keep a hint of a smile on your face in a very relaxed manner.

Body positioning

When you are building Comfort with her, turn your body to face hers directly. Look attentive and like you are fully invested in the interaction. Lean forward when you get really engrossed in what she is saying. When you are building Attraction and showing value, it's ok to lean back and talk at a slight angle to her; but in Comfort, turn your body so it faces her completely.

Touching

Touching a woman builds Comfort with her. Touch her hand or her arm when you are talking and want to emphasize an emotion behind a point, for example, "Oh my god, I went on the best rollercoaster the other day [touch her arm lightly]; you would have loved it!"

Stroke her arm while you are sitting next to her or in front of her. Take her hand and hold it when you move from one place to another. Stroke strands of her hair back over her face. Give her a kiss on the forehead or cheek every now and then. Finally, a nice gesture that demonstrates a protective and strong quality is to put your arm around her lower back whenever there is a crowd of people bustling by.

Logistical comfort

How well we feel like we know someone is not just a function of time but a function of memories shared as well. Therefore the more different places you see and different things you do with a woman, the more memories and Comfort you create with her.

Logistical Comfort includes the following:

- **Instant-dating.** Moving her from where you first met her in the daytime to another location. Walking with a woman down the street is the simplest example of an instant date that builds Comfort. If that goes well, you could take a longer walk around the city (if it's a decent area and a good day to walk), go to a park, grab a coffee or a drink.

- **Going on a date in the evening.** Meeting her again later that evening or a few days after you first met her is the most frequently used method of building logistical Comfort.

- **Venue changing.** Taking her to a few different bars when you go on a date is sometimes preferable to just staying in one bar for three hours, because more memories are created from being with you in three different environments rather than just one.

- **Doing activities together.** This can be as simple as dancing together in a night club, doing shots at the bar, cooking together or watching a DVD at home. As you get deeper into Comfort (once you in a relationship), the activities can include meeting each other's friends and families or taking a trip away together.

Signs of comfort

Addressing how much Comfort you need to build with each individual woman is more difficult: although there are certain signals you can look out for, they are never 100% foolproof and women will always surprise you with how ready or not they are to get more physical with you.

Nevertheless, here are some good signs that indicate you have a decent level of Comfort:

- She tells you personal things about her that she wouldn't tell to strangers.

- She leaves her friends to spend time with you or comes out by herself to meet you (including coming on a date with you).

- She agrees to do things for you. For example, cook for you, wear a sexy outfit for you, or bring wine over to your place.

- She agrees to do things with you. For example, come to a dance lesson with you, watch a DVD with you, or come to a party with you.

Ultimately though, the only way you know whether you have enough Comfort is to try to progress and observe the response. If you try to progress and she complies or reciprocates then you have enough Comfort. If she doesn't, then you need to build more Comfort.

For example, if you ask her if she wants to come back to your place, or she is at your place and you try to take her clothes off, any of the following responses indicate that you don't have enough Comfort with her:

- This is moving too fast.

- I don't know you that well.

- Can we just talk?

- We need to slow down.

If you get a response like this, it's not a big deal. It's not the woman rejecting you or any reason to feel disappointed at all. All the woman is saying is that you need to build some more Comfort with her first. So simply keep talking and using the methods described in the rest of this chapter to build more Comfort and try progressing again a little later.

Chapter summary

- Comfort is the phase when you and a woman get to know each other on a more personal level.

- It is achieved by mutual sharing and empathizing on personal topics. Building deeper Comfort means talking about things that involve more intense emotions.

- You can build Comfort in verbal, physical and logistical ways.

- You know you have built enough Comfort when she is comfortable with you progressing things (physically and/or logistically).

DAYTIME DATING: Never Sleep Alone

PART III
PHYSICAL AND LOGISTICAL PROGRESSION

Chapter 11: Physical Progression

What is physical progression?

In the last part of the book we looked at how to talk with a woman to build emotional intimacy with her (the Emotional Progression part of the Love Systems Triad). But you also need to understand Physical and Logistical Progression if you are going to sleep with her.

Physical Progression means advancing through more intimate levels of physical contact with a woman; for example kissing or sleeping with her. Logistical Progression is about getting her alone (away from friends) and somewhere private where you can get more intimate with her.

It's natural to find these two aspects of seduction challenging. Most men experience a similar fear of rejection when they consider kissing a woman, asking her out or when they consider approaching a woman. The progression steps outlined in this chapter are fairly straightforward; the challenge lies mainly in overcoming your anxieties and being willing to "risk" taking things further with a woman.

If you are building Attraction, Qualification and Comfort, a woman expects and hopes that you will progress the interaction with her. In fact, if you don't, she will lose some attraction for you. Conversely, if you try to progress things with her and you don't succeed – perhaps she declines your offer of a coffee or says, "I can't right now" – her Attraction to you actually increases because you had the guts to lead and try to take things further. She may even be attracted to you quite a bit, but is not completely ready yet – so you need to spend more time building Attraction, Qualification and Comfort with her.

Physical progression in daytime dating

The principles described in Magic Bullets for Physical and Logistical Progression largely apply to daytime dating as well as in bars and clubs, but the major difference to bear in mind is:

- Physical touching should be kept light until you are on a date with her

In a nighttime venue, a higher level of touching is socially acceptable and even expected. But in the daytime, excessive touching can intimidate a woman. That's not to say you shouldn't touch her at all. Using Social Touch (and in some cases, Friendly Touch) is a really good idea, but you want to save the more intimate forms of Physical Progression for when you are on a date with her or somewhere private.

Physical progression steps

The surprising truth of women is that they enjoy sex as much as we do (if not more so), but the route they prefer to get there is different. As men, we tend to think in concrete, pre-planned and logical steps; for example, "We like each other, therefore we should go home together and have sex." Women prefer to feel that things are flowing naturally from one event to the next, almost beyond their control – which is why they frequently use the phrase, "one thing led to another," to describe dates that end in sex.

The secret to Physical Progression is to make the steps as small as possible. If you haven't touched her for three hours, then suddenly you lunge forward to kiss her as your date ends, she will be taken by surprise and probably recoil. On the other hand, if you've been sitting close to her, gradually touching her hands, her arms and hair more and more over the last few hours, then it will seem natural to turn her head and kiss her a little on the lips.

The second part of it is that every time you take a step forward, you are testing whether she is ready or not. Of course if you are building Attraction, Qualification and Comfort then a woman should be attracted to you, but you never 100% know if she is ready to progress the interaction with you until you try. So be willing to make a small step forward to see how she reacts.

If a woman lets you touch her or doesn't recoil from your touch, then that's almost certainly a green light that says, "I am comfortable and enjoy you touching me like this." If she does pull back or look uncomfortable, then slow down for a little while, concentrate on your Emotional Progression (Attraction, Qualification and Comfort) and wait until a little later to try touching her again.

When you make these little steps forward physically, you will probably feel some anxiety. You might think, "What if she rejects my advance? Will she be angry with me or lose Attraction for me?" The reality of it is that if you are talking to a woman and showing value, she expects that you will try to take the interaction further. You hurt yourself more by not doing so – because you show that you don't have the confidence to lead and take risks with her. Countless times a woman has spurned my advances, only for us to keep conversing and later end up being physical with each other.

There are four stages of physical progression: Social, Friendly, Romantic and Sexual Touch. We covered these already in the Love Systems Triad chapter, but let's have a look in greater detail at how to apply these when we meet women during the daytime.

Social Touch

Social Touch should be used immediately after approaching a woman in the daytime. In fact, it's a part of the Bridge process: you shake her hand as you exchange names with her.

Beyond the handshake, however, it can be very powerful to use light touches on her hand, forearm, elbow or shoulder from time to time as you talk to her over the next few minutes. These light touches get her used to having a level of physical contact with you and will reinforce the Emotional Progression you do with her, especially if you use them during peaks of emotional intensity in the conversation.

The light touch can be difficult to master but is incredibly useful if you do. Think of it like how you would smile at certain points while telling an exciting story to someone or when someone is telling you about something that made them happy. The smile reinforces the emotional peak. You can use a light touch on the arm to achieve the same thing.

Here are a couple of examples where the light touch could be used while you are saying things to her, indicated in square brackets []:

- Oh my God, I have to tell you about something that happened to me today. It was crazy! [touch]

- I know that not everyone would make the decision that I made. I feel like there were a lot of people that advised me against taking the risk. Honestly though [touch], I'm glad I did because I've never been happier.

- Sarah, I think it's incredible how passionate you are about life. I love that about you [touch].

Friendly Touch

Friendly Touch, such as cheek kissing or hugging, is best used when you've established some level of Comfort with a woman.

This might not happen within the first five minutes of meeting her, but that's a not a problem. When you go on a date with her, you can start Social Touch again and then progress into Friendly Touch soon after that.

In some cases, you will get along so well with a woman as soon as you meet her that it might feel more natural to give her a hug goodbye or otherwise use some kind of Friendly Touch. That's fine, but don't go overboard with it (otherwise you'll come off as creepy). If you're unsure, it's best to just wait until you get her on a date.

Romantic Touch

Romantic Touch, such as stroking her hair or holding hands, should generally be used when you're on a date with a woman or somewhere private.

In some cases during a daytime approach, a woman will allow you to do these things – and maybe even kiss her on the lips – but this can sometimes hurt your chances of sleeping with her later on, especially if you haven't built much Comfort with her yet. So for the most part, it's safest to wait until you're on a date with her to use Romantic Touch.

When you're on the date, try to sit next to her on a couch or some kind of continuous seating arrangement instead of on separate chairs. Definitely try to avoid sitting across a table from her. You want to be physically close to her, and be able to increase that closeness as you talk more without it being awkward.

Start gently with a few lingering touches on her hands or arms, and then gradually hold your touches for a little longer each time. If there's no resistance or flinching on her part, progress to touching the tips of her hair or stroking a little bit of it back over her ear.

If you get to this point with a woman and there's still no resistance, she is most likely thinking about kissing you. Move in slowly; if she doesn't move back or flinch, go in to kiss her on the lips.

However, don't kiss her for too long. Pull back soon after and keep talking. If you make out with her for a long time, it dissipates the sexual tension and she won't be as excited about coming home with you when you try to logistically progress things. Sometimes, you can get a woman to come back to your place without even having kissed her on the date.

Magic Bullets has an excellent chapter that goes into more detail on the best ways to kiss a woman and the pitfalls to avoid – if you're not experienced with kissing women, I highly recommend it.

Sexual Touching

Sexual Touching (which includes anything beyond kissing) should only begin when you are somewhere private with a woman.

From here on in, it is about getting her turned on with your ability to stimulate her physically, taking each other's clothes off and becoming fully intimate.

Remember that it's still your responsibility to lead and progress things. Don't wait for her to take her clothes off or suggest you have sex. Start by touching her more intimately; for example, kissing her more passionately and touching her breasts or rubbing her thighs.

As she gets more turned on, you can start to take her clothes and yours off. This is not a sex manual, so you're on your own from this point!

Chapter summary

- Trying to progress things with a woman rarely decreases her Attraction for you, but can often increase it.

- There are four stages of Physical Progression: Social Touch, Friendly Touch.

- Romantic Touch and Sexual Touch. In the initial daytime approach, you only really need to focus on Social Touch.

- Once you are on a date with a woman, you can do more Friendly Touch and possibly some Romantic Touch.

- When you are in a place where you can sleep together (typically your place or her place), you can do more Romantic Touch and begin Sexual Touch.

Chapter 12: Logistical Progression

What is logistical progression?

Logistical Progression describes the planning, execution and control of moving from place to place while you are with a woman. Remember how physically, she wants things to progress smoothly from one step to another? It is the same with how you progress things logistically.

It would be a large jump to expect her to go from having met you on the street in the afternoon, to coming back to your place thirty minutes later (though it is not impossible). More likely, there would be a series of smaller Logistical Progression steps in between to make the process smoother.

Logistical progression in daytime dating

The major difference for Logistical Progression between daytime dating and meeting women at night is:

- Women are less likely to be logistically available immediately.

When you meet a woman in a bar or nightclub, if you know what you're doing you have a reasonable chance of taking her home that night. In the daytime, it's less likely she'll be available to come home with you in that instance. Chances are she will have stuff to do soon after you approach her or otherwise have plans for the rest of the afternoon. So in many cases, you will have to set up a date for a later time and take her phone number.

There are two major options for Logistical Progression in daytime dating: Traditional Dates and Instant Dates. Let's take a look at both of these in more detail.

Traditional dates

The fact is that a lot of the women you talk to in the daytime will be busy shopping, running errands, on their way to meet people and so forth. It would be great if you are getting along with a woman to be able to spend time with her straightaway, but it won't always happen.

A lot of the time, therefore, you will need to arrange to meet her another time and take her contact details. The phone number is not the goal here; setting up the date is the goal.

Ideally, you want to see her in an evening sometime soon so you can talk more over drinks. Meeting for drinks in the evening is a good low-risk date that allows intimacy to develop. Dinner is too intense for a first date for a lot of people, and things like movies don't allow you to focus on the conversational aspect of the date (i.e. Emotional Progression).

So if you've approached a woman in the daytime and had a good conversation for a few minutes – one in which you've built some Attraction and Qualification – then ask her if she'd like to talk more over a drink. The emphasis should be on the two of you talking more, rather than you "taking her out" or "buying her dinner."

The easiest way to ask a woman out is to use some Qualification and then follow it with a logistical suggestion.

For example:

- I've really enjoyed talking to you for the last few minutes. How would you feel about grabbing a drink sometime and finding out more about each other?

- It's great that you're into [some topic that you've discussed with her and both enjoyed]. I'd love to talk to you more sometime. How do you feel about a coffee or a drink sometime soon?

- I think you're the sort of person I could click pretty well with. If you're free some time this week, would you like to talk more over a drink?

If she agrees, then set up a rough time and place to meet her. The sooner the better, so if she's free that evening, that's ideal. If not, see how available she is over the next few nights. Then take her phone number so you can confirm again with her closer to the time.

If I sense that she might not be comfortable or attracted enough yet when I ask her out, I might suggest a "coffee or a drink" rather than just suggesting a drink, to see what she bites on. Some women you meet might not accept a drink after a short conversation with you, but might agree to a coffee as its less investment on their part.

If she declines, then thank her for the conversation and move on. It's really that simple. To be successful with women, you need to realise that sometimes a woman will just not be into you, or will be into you but not available to meet with you (perhaps she has a boyfriend or perhaps she really is too busy right now). There are plenty of women out there, so don't focus on converting everyone who turns you down; instead, find the women that do want to date you.

Instant dates

An Instant Date is when you try to spend more time with a woman very soon after meeting her, instead of a Traditional Date where you arrange to meet again another time. An Instant Date could mean walking down the street together for a while, stopping for coffee, heading to a bar nearby or even going back to your place.

Instant Dates are great if you both have time to do that when you meet. They work really well with approaches done in the early evening, when women are more likely to be able to come to a bar with you straightaway, or with women who have the day off from work or are on holiday.

The important things to bear in mind for Instant Dating are:

- Ask logistical questions like, "What are you doing today?" and "What are your plans for tonight?" to establish her availability. The firmer her existing plans, the less likely it is she can spend time with you straightaway.

- Make your logistical progression steps as small and linear as possible.

- Moving from a coffee shop to your place an hour away is a big jump, but coffee, a bar a few minutes away, a cab ride to a restaurant, and finally a five-minute walk back to your place is a series of smaller, linear steps.

- Make it seem like a spontaneous adventure. It shouldn't feel like you have a pre-planned "game plan" that you normally take women through. The way to avoid this is to genuinely avoid having a set logistical plan that you always use. Be creative and do things that you enjoy instead of trying to create the perfect logistical sequence. If you feel like visiting a certain place that you think will be fun for both of you, go for it.

When you suggest moving somewhere, show some Qualification of your interaction so far and suggest a small next step so that you can get to know each other better. On the big steps (for example, coming back to your place), it can be a good idea to include an "out" for her so she doesn't feel pressured. For example, if you invite her back to your place, you can tell her you'll call a cab for her if it gets late or that you'll walk her back to a bus or train stop.

Here are some examples of things to say to progress things logistically:

- I'm really enjoying this conversation with you. Which way are you headed? I'll walk with you for a few minutes so we can find out some more about each other.

- You seem like a really cool person. What are you doing right now? Nothing? How do you feel about grabbing a quick cup of coffee and talking some more? There's a place right around the corner.

- I can't believe I just met you an hour ago and here we are drinking coffee. I feel like you and have so much in common. Do you have anywhere you need to be? No? Let's go grab a drink for a bit – there's a really cool bar near here I know.

- I have bottle of wine back at my place. Do you want to come for a glass? I can walk you back to the train station afterwards.

Chapter summary

- After meeting a woman for five minutes in the daytime, you can either ask her out on a Traditional Date, or go for an Instant Date. Instant Dates will only work when you both have lots of time to spend with each other right there and then, so in a lot of cases you will end up going for Traditional Dates.

- Set up a Traditional Date for an evening within the next couple of days ideally. Arrange to meet at a bar and have drinks together. Avoid dinner, movies or any other date ideas people have told you.

DAYTIME DATING: Never Sleep Alone

Chapter 13: Case Studies

Now that you understand how to emotionally, physically, and logistically progress things with a woman you meet in the daytime, let's look at some case studies that put all this information together.

Read the following two stories, told from both the male and female perspective and try to pick out the elements you've learned from this book within them. Both of these are the sort of things that will happen to you if you practice everything taught to you in this book (they are both based on typical situations I've experienced).

After that, I've included one of my personal stories and a daytime dating adventure from a friend of mine.

Enjoy.

John and Sarah – John's story

I met Sarah on the street – she was walking past me and it turns out she was on her way to meet some friends for lunch. She was so captivating that I had to stop her and find out some more about her. We ended up having a really interesting conversation about her travelling to Spain to become a chef and a few other things. It struck me that here was a woman who was beautiful, ambitious, independent and passionate about things in her life. That's my kind of woman and I knew that she was worth getting to know better.

After talking for about ten minutes, it seemed like she was eager to end the conversation - suddenly I remembered that she had said she was on her way to have lunch with her friends. She was in a rush, so rather than continue talking to her, I told her that I thought she was interesting and that I'd love to get a coffee or drink with her sometime. She liked the idea and told me that she was free for a drink tomorrow night. That worked for my schedule, so we swapped numbers and I told her I'd text her later on. I texted later that evening, "Any other charming strangers stop you on the street today? ;-) Looking forward to drinks tomorrow," to tease her a little and make her think about me later on in the day.

We met up the next night at a great bar near my place and got along famously. We shared a bottle of wine and then I took her to another bar where I know the manager. I chatted with him a bit and then got us some more drinks. As I listened to Sarah talking and looked at her, I realized that I wanted to sleep with her. She was really sweet and funny; she opened up to me about the things she wanted to do in life and what was important to her in the people she met.

She totally met my standards for a high quality woman, so I invited her back to my place for a cup of coffee and told her I'd call her a cab later on. She never needed the cab and stayed the night with me.

John and Sarah – Sarah's story

I was rushing to meet my girlfriends for lunch when I felt someone tap me on the arm and say, "Excuse me." I turned around and there was a guy standing there looking at me with his eyes wide open, as if he'd just seen something amazing. He said something about how he loved my outfit and the way I walked. I was really surprised – I've almost never had a guy (especially a well-dressed cute guy like this one) stop me on the street like that.

He started asking me questions about what I did and what sort of things I was into. He was really relaxed and confident, which made me comfortable enough to tell him a bit more about myself. It was strange: even though he said I was attractive, it was like he was trying to figure out whether he liked me or not. Most guys normally just hit on me outright, especially in nightclubs, and then try to impress me by telling me how good their job is or how much money they earn.

I didn't actually find out that much about him in those first few minutes. He had a wonderful way of making me laugh, being confident and talking generally about things that it didn't even cross my mind to ask him what he did for a living, whether he was single, or whatever else. I just felt drawn to him by his presence.

I really had to get going, so we talked briefly about a date and he took my number. I really didn't know what to expect of it after that. For all I knew, he was a player and did this all the time. I thought he probably wasn't going to call me. Then I got this funny text from him that evening that made me smile, and I started looking forward to seeing him again.

When we went out for drinks the next night, he was just as interesting and charming as he was when I first met him, even more so in fact. I could tell he was a guy who had choice and freedom in his life, and it flattered me that he thought so highly of me – he kept on saying the most intuitive and complimentary things about me.

I got really attracted to him and was hoping he'd ask me to come back to his place. I didn't want to feel like a slut though, so I was really grateful when he suggested that we just have a quick coffee and then he'd call me a cab. When we were on his couch, I could feel all the sexual tension bubbling up from the past few hours. He was talking to me but I just kept looking at his lips and hoping he'd kiss me. Then he reached over and touched my hair a little bit. It almost gave me goose pimples.

Finally, he leaned over and we kissed, softly and gently at first. Then he took my hand and we went to his bedroom, where I spent the night. I'd like to see him again, but honestly if he didn't call me, I wouldn't be upset. I've never had a date as good as that and he was an amazing lover.

Ravi and Anna – Ravi's story

I met Anna in the bookstore. I was browsing the cookery section when I saw her on the other side next to the travel books. She looked like an angel, so I went over and paid her a compliment on her hair. She was really easy going and we started chatting about where she was from – it turns out she had recently moved here from Norway.

We talked a bit about moving to different countries, how she was enjoying London, and what the differences between Norwegian and English men were. It was hilarious: she told me that a Norwegian guy would never come up to her like I did. I teased her and told her I only approached her because I saw her checking me out, and that I bet she comes to bookstores all the time to pick up guys.

She told me she was just browsing guidebooks for London and doing a little shopping today; she had plans later tonight though. I was enjoying talking to her – she had a beauty that I hadn't seen in a while, and she was confident and intelligent. So I told her to come over and help me choose a good cookbook from the other section of the store.

We started having some fun with it. I told her I was a world-class chef and that if she was a good girl, she could be my sous chef. We were having such a good time that I suggested that we take a walk and that she didn't need a London guidebook because she had me now.

We went for a walk around the city and I showed her a couple of the cool things I like in London. We'd stop off for coffee or food every now and then and I got to find out a lot more about her. Aside from being incredibly sexy, she was also artistic, smart and really open-minded – definitely my kind of woman.

It was starting to get towards evening time and I remembered that she had plans later tonight. So I suggested a quick drink at a great bar I know that was really close to my place. I kept on joking with her that she had to sample my cooking and then said at the very least she had to try one of my beautiful cups of coffee.

After the bar, we went back to my place and starting making out like crazy once we got inside. She suddenly got cold feet and told me, "I can't do this, I barely know you." I realized that maybe I had moved too fast. So I told her it was cool and that we could just talk for a while.

We sat on my bed and she started opening up to me that she'd never done this sort of thing before and that a lot of her previous boyfriends were successful guys but were really needy. I empathized with her and told her it was hard to find good, confident and secure people – and that was one of the reasons why I liked her so much.

Twenty minutes later she started kissing me again and then reached for my trousers. We had intense and passionate sex before her phone started ringing off the hook – I guess it was her friends calling her.

Afterwards, she left with a huge smile on her face and rushed out to go meet her friends. I definitely want to see her again.

Ravi and Anna – Anna's story

Today was crazy. Some guy started talking to me in the bookstore and I ended up having sex with him. I still don't know exactly how it happened – one thing just seemed to lead to another.

I was standing in the travel section when he just came up to me, told me he liked my hair and started talking with me. He had this amazing confidence and a great sense of humor. He kept on messing around with me pretending he was a world famous chef; it was pretty funny. But he also seemed to be an all-round interesting guy with lots going on in his life. I like that in a man: he has to be driven and have things that are important to him beyond just a girlfriend or a woman. A lot of my boyfriends in the past have been so needy.

One moment we were in the bookstore, the next he was taking me on a tour of London. It was so much fun! He showed me lots of things I've never seen before and took me to this cool little bar. I started to feel so attracted to him, but wasn't sure what was going to happen. I don't normally sleep with guys on the first date, let alone a guy I just met in the bookstore! But there was something so charming and fun-loving about him that made me feel comfortable being with him. He was clearly a guy who took risks in his life, and I guess that made me want to take a risk as well.

I agreed to come to his place for a cup of coffee. I thought if he started being creepy or needy, I would just leave. I really wanted to kiss him and we started making out when we got inside. But then I started to feel uncomfortable so I stopped him.

Was this common for him? Did he do it all the time? I didn't want to be just another girl he had sex with. He said he was okay for us to just talk and he seemed to be a great listener. I told him about my previous boyfriends and why I didn't like them. Just from the way he was listening and the things he said to me I could tell he wasn't like any of those guys: I knew he wanted to sleep with me, but he didn't seem to mind if it didn't happen.

That turned me on so much and I knew I wanted him in that instant. I was late to dinner with the girls in the end, but it was well worth it! I left him my number and I hope he calls. He seemed like the kind of guy that isn't looking for a girlfriend, but I'd be happy to just be friends or keep it casual for a while. I'm not really looking for a boyfriend right now either.

The Spanish Brunette – Jeremy Soul's story

I was cruising the streets with a good friend of mine, talking but keeping an eye out for beautiful girls. I had already talked with a few girls that afternoon, and gotten a few numbers, but I wanted to meet someone really beautiful that I could spend some time with that day.

I noticed two girls quickly walk past us, a tall, slim brunette, and a short, not-so-hot blonde girl. I looked back at them as they passed me, so I could get a good look.

The brunette girl turned her head, and looked back at me. She was stunningly beautiful. I stopped, and held her gaze for a few seconds. She looked slightly confused, so I waved back to her in a friendly and slightly cheeky way. She looked even more confused, and they kept on walking.

It's moments like this that define the kind of life you lead. There are two types of guy in the world. The first type will let his emotions, in particular, fear, control his actions. This is a guy who does not take risks, and will therefore never achieve the kind of success he wants in life.

The second type feels the fear in exactly the same way, but is willing to take action in spite of how he feels inside. He is a risk taker, and realizes that he needs to challenge the unknown in order to get what he wants from life. His mind may want to make certain assumptions about situations – for example, "That girl is out of my league" – but he will challenge all negative assumptions with his action rather than allow them to dictate his actions.

I didn't know what this beautiful woman was thinking when she looked back at me. She might have thought she recognized me, she might have thought I was cute, or she might have thought, "Wow, that guy is ugly!" I had no idea, but I wasn't going to let her pass me by without finding out.

I ran back towards the two girls, tapped them both on the shoulder, and said to the beautiful brunette,

"Excuse me, I just saw you walking past and you are so beautiful that I had to come over and say hello. I couldn't just let you walk past!"

Then I turned to the not-so-good looking friend, and said, "You are very lovely too, but I have a thing for tall brunettes!"

It took me a long time to be able to say sentences like this with confidence and to make them work. Believe me, saying this sort of stuff to random women on the street does take guts, but that is exactly what women find so attractive about it. In this case, I also had to pay some attention to the friend, so that I wouldn't make the social situation awkward. Also, I wanted the friend to think I was cool and interesting, so that she could say, "He's cool," to her friend later on.

Both girls had stopped walking and turned to face me. This was the first positive signal. They were allowing me to interact with them. If they hadn't stopped and just ignored me and carried on, I would have gone and talked to some other girls. Some guys try to convince girls to like them after they have clearly shown they're not interested. This is a waste of your time that could be better spent finding girls that do like you.

I asked them what they were doing today and made small talk for a few seconds. Then I told the beautiful girl again that she was beautiful, had lovely hair, and was dressed so elegantly that I couldn't help but notice her. I also teased her by accusing her of looking at me when I walked past because she thought I was cute.

She denied it, and said she thought she recognized me. I told her with a wink and a smile that she was a good liar. Everything I said, I said with a smile on my face. My goal was just to make her giggle a few times. Once I could do that, I knew she would feel comfortable around me and start to like me.

I talked about what I was doing out with my friend that day, what I did in London, and about the kinds of people that I liked to meet. Most guys are afraid to talk about themselves when they meet girls. Women make them nervous and all they can think to do is ask lots of questions. Screw that! To get women attracted to you, you have to lead an interesting life and be willing to talk about it.

I talked to them for a few minutes, and then said, "Hey, I have to go, but I would really like to speak with you some more," at which point she enthusiastically said, "You should take my number!" As she put her number into my phone, I made a few more jokes with the blonde friend. I told her that the brunette was very good at this, and I bet she does this all the time. The brunette started giggling again, and said, "You're crazy, but I like it."

I told her we should meet up tonight so we can get to know each other better, and she smiled and said, "Yes, call me!"

This was on. I could tell this was going to be a solid date. I texted a couple of hours later saying, "Hey beautiful, great to meet you earlier today in the street. Let's go out for drinks tonight, can you meet me at [easy meeting point in town] at X time?"

She replied and agreed to meet up. I met her at 11pm that night and gave her a hug as we met. I suggested that we could go out to a bar later, but that I had some wine in my apartment that we could drink before going out. She said, "Good idea."

At this point, I felt she was so attracted to me that I didn't even need to take her out to a bar. I just needed to get her to my place so I could seduce her. However, I told her, "We'll go out to a bar later," to reassure her so that if she felt uncomfortable, we would still have that option.

We get in a taxi and head back to my place. Once there, I pour her some wine, talk and get to know her for about twenty minutes. I then kiss her and lead her by the hand into my bedroom.

We make love, and I lie next to her and get to know her some more afterwards. If you want to see a woman again, you have to make sure she feels safe, comfortable and appreciated after you've had sex for the first time.

She is probably one of the most beautiful and charming women I have ever met in my life, and it all happened because I decided to take a chance when I saw her walk past me that day. You never know what could happen until you try.

Airport Pick Up – Leko's story

I have to admit that I was one of those guys for which day game seemed impossible. Even after a long time in the dating community and a good level of expertise, 100% of my closes came from the nighttime, in bars and clubs.

I just wasn't able to gather the courage to speak to a girl during the day. In fact, it was like a trip back in time to my chump days. I couldn't think of things to say, thus I didn't approach. I was a classic werewolf: fearsome and irresistible at night, but a plain, timid man during the day.

I had met Soul on a bootcamp in Stockholm. We clicked instantly and I visited him one night in London. We went to a club and both scored, but he had met his girl during the day and I met mine at night. It was the second time I had seen him take home a girl he'd met some hours before but I had never seen the actual procedure.

Then, he came to Barcelona to repay me the visit. He arrived with a friend and we were all starving, so we went to eat a pizza. What followed has never ceased to astonish me. We took forty minutes to walk the five blocks from my place to the restaurant. Every time we saw a beautiful girl, Soul disappeared and went to talk to her in less time than it takes to think, "Wow, that chick is hot, I should talk to her!"

He number closed five of them. It was more than the total number I opened during the day in my whole life! That's when my actual day game initiation started. I picked his brain mercilessly and carefully watched every approach he made. And he was a fantastic teacher, sharing his knowledge and explaining to me every step of his theory. I would never stop being grateful to him for that.

Fast forward one year. I had still picked up most of my girls at night. It's my specialty, after all. But my game was much more balanced. And I had tested Soul's techniques dozens of times in the field with fantastic success. I even adapted them to suit my style. That summer I went to London and went daytime approaching with him again. He still was the best of the best, but this time I wasn't that far behind.

Only some weeks later I went to Vienna on holiday for a couple of days. I went to Budapest to party and then back to Barcelona on a flight that departed at 6am. I was abso lutely knackered. When I got on the plane all I wanted was to get to my seat and sleep. I always sit in the back of planes, because they are usually emptier and I can see if there are any hot girls on my way there. This time, I saw one in one of the front rows and thought, "Wow, she's cute". But I was too tired, so I went back and slept for the whole two hours.

When we landed, the girl walked past by again. Fuck, she wasn't just cute, she was one of the hottest girls I've ever seen. She was 6 feet tall with model looks. A 10. I sat in front of her in the shuttle to the airport and thought, "I definitely have to talk to this girl."

But I couldn't do it right away. There were too many people around which made the situation too high-pressured. And I knew she wasn't going anywhere anyway. So I waited for her to pick up her luggage and decided to approach after she crossed the door to the airport hallway.

I never realized that was a big mistake. What if there was someone waiting for her? The pick-up gods smiled at me this time though: she crossed the hall by herself. (Funnily, it was she who pointed this out to me some days later). So I rushed to her, steadied myself before opening and said the trademark phrase, "Excuse me, I usually don 't do this but I thought you were super sexy and wanted to talk to you."

Usually, they laugh and say thank you. In this case her answer was, "Ok, is that it?" Bang! That took me out of the script. That made me fumble my next line but fortunately all the practice I had helped me recover. Disregarding what she just said, I kept on going with my opening. "Ermm.. but it's not just that, you're really tall and have a fantastic style, you have to be a model."

She wasn't, but that line is gold. Every girl will be flattered with that comparison and then she gave me a break. She asked me if I spoke Spanish, so I quickly switched and I started building on that. After five minutes of conversation I asked her if she wanted to have a coffee with me right then. I knew she had three hours to wait for her connection so she wouldn't say no.

So, we were on an instant date. As it usually happens in these cases I talked, a lot. But little by little she started opening up and I discovered a bright girl behind those astonishing looks. We talked about nothing and everything and the time flew by. When she had to leave I felt there was a fantastic chemistry mounting, but well... she had to leave and my calibration sense told me I could just go for a number and email close at that moment.

So I sent her an email three days after that. No answer. No problem. I had other girls to take care of and I knew I played good game; she would eventually look for me. She did and after a week and a half. She had a layover of nine hours in Barcelona for her flight back, and asked if I wanted to show her the night life.

Of course I wanted to! We went out, had a fantastic night and ended up in my bed. The chemistry was so good that I almost made her miss her flight! Since that moment, we are really close. I fly to Vienna once every two months and she does the same to Barcelona. She came with me to New York and I will join her on a ski trip. We have since decided to go exclusive and, surprisingly for a guy whose had six multiple relationships at one time, I feel really comfortable with it. And nothing of this would have had happened if it wasn't for Soul and his passion for day game.

Cheers mate.

Leko

Conclusion

You now have enough information to meet and date all the women you could ever want to in the daytime. But unless you go out and actually practice what you have learned, this is going to be just another book that you read and store somewhere.

I've met countless people in my time as a coach for Love Systems who knew all the right information and what they had to do, but never actually did it.

People always ask successful men, "How did you become so successful?" The answer is hard work. The difference between the successful and the unsuccessful is that we have the guts to try something, and then to keep trying even when it doesn't quite work how we had hoped the first time. Eventually things start slotting into place, and before you know it, you have the lifestyle and the women in your life that you once dreamed you would have.

Finally, if you need any more help, whether you're looking for live training or any other good resources, we're always here at www.lovesystems.com .

Hit me up on my facebook page with any comments or feedback you have on the book.

BONUS CHAPTERS

Introduction to Approach Anxiety

I hope that not only do you really enjoy reading this and learning from it, but that you see a major shift in the way you view "cold approach" (meeting women that you haven't met before) going forward.

The concepts and ideas in this book came not only from painful personal experiences as I struggled with my shyness and my fragile ego in my early days, but more than anything they are a compilation of common sense ideas and collective experiences of many, many men before you and me.

Even though "approaching" is only a small part of the Love Systems Triad Model, it is consistently the one area that guys state as their biggest challenge when they arrive for our Bootcamps...only to find out how easily they get over this on their very first night and realize that it is actually one of the easiest things they learn during the weekend...and this is what drove me to put this together.

When was the last time you saw a beautiful woman, but either did not have the courage to talk to her or made up some excuse as to why you shouldn't?

Probably quite recently – if you are being truly honest – and perhaps even earlier today?

Let's make something very clear right up front – approach anxiety is normal and approach anxiety is good. In fact most Love Systems instructors will admit that they still feel approach anxiety – particularly on their first approach of the day or evening. It is a signal that you are doing something right – that you are moving beyond your comfort zone – and that is exactly what you should be doing if you are going to grow and experience new and incredible things.

This article is aimed at two types of people:

1. Newbies who need a helping hand to get out of the starting gate.
2. More experienced guys who are maybe not pushing their dating skill as far as they could and should.

What I have tried to provide you with is as follows:

a. Background to approach anxiety – what it is and why it is so natural.
b. Logical explanations for why it is so important to approach and get out of your comfort zone.
c. Practical tips on how to actually start approaching.

Good luck and have fun!

Carbeau

Love Systems Instructor

Chapter 14: What is Approach Anxiety?

Fear of approach or "approach anxiety" are simply labels we use to describe natural physiological responses that our bodies generate when taking risks – specifically increased blood flow in the amygdale, a core part of the brain that performs a primary role in the processing of emotional reactions. If anyone has engaged in activities, such as skydiving, bungee jumping, and extreme skiing or simply taken a major rollercoaster ride, then you will recognize a similar feeling. It is hard-wired into our genetic programming – we feel it whenever we face a challenge, test our boundaries or break our comfort zones...

How modern social programming complicates things...

Artificial modern social norms that have developed over the past 50-100 years have been responsible for exacerbating feelings of anxiety, particularly in more hierarchical and conformist societies, such as in East Asia and Northern Europe. Modern social programming has conditioned many of us to shy away from cold approaching women for a host of reasons, such as:

- Modern fears of kidnap / pedophilia, etc. have trained children not to talk to strangers.

- Modern urban lifestyle conditions people to keep to themselves and not talk to strangers (when was the last time you talked to a stranger on the bus / metro / underground?).

- Modern social focus on privacy conditions us to respect other people's personal space.

- Increasingly litigious society causes men to fear civil or criminal legal proceedings for "harassment."

- Fear of damaging your reputation / being known as a "sleaze ball" within a limited social circle.

- Fear of rejection / injury to personal ego.

This social programming pushes us to seek safe ground rather than taking risks and has made it increasingly difficult for us to tap into our natural biological desire to push our boundaries (think about how, as young boys, we sought to climb higher trees or jump off higher diving boards). We literally need to peel away the layers of social programming that hold us back and get back to our natural biological programming. Instead of allowing any one of the above reasons to become a convenient excuse for taking the safe route (i.e. not approaching), we need to embrace the experience and feel the rush of positive emotions that we experience when we venture just beyond our comfort zone.

Chapter 15: Why should you approach women?

It is part of your DNA – embrace it, don't fight it!

Learning to "overcome" approach anxiety is like learning to overcome the need to eat or sleep. Studies have shown that, in the absence of challenge, men can become clinically depressed – facing and dealing with challenge is core to our male essence – living life within your comfort zone is contrary to our natural biological state.

Remember that your biological purpose is just two things: to survive and replicate – no more than. So anything leading to replication is absolutely core to your sense of self and your masculine identity in particular and will feed you emotionally – therefore you don't want to overcome approach anxiety, you want to embrace each challenge and re-connect with your biological imperative. Once you do this a few times in quick succession (and gain momentum), you will enter a virtuous cycle of risk and reward – each time you approach and push your boundaries, you will get such a rush that it will make you hungry for the next one. Trust me.

Take action and get your dopamine hit!

The only way to move from paralysis to taking action is...by taking action!

Taking action in order to take action is a chicken and egg paradox to some extent. However, when we take action, our brains release a neurotransmitter chemical, dopamine, which is designed to make us feel good, producing effects such as increased heart rate and blood pressure.

In fact, dopamine is believed to provide a teaching signal to parts of the brain responsible for acquiring new behavior. Since dopamine neurons are observed when an unexpected reward is presented, they encode a conditioned stimulus after repeated pairings with a specific reward. Thus dopamine helps us learn to repeat behaviors that maximize rewards.

Have you ever grudgingly washed your car or cleaned the kitchen and found that you feel great once you get going? That's the dopamine kicking in.

Nobody can reject you based on a cold approach

Think about this - a woman does not know you and has no idea what kind of guy you are when you approach and therefore, if she blows you out, she is not rejecting you, she is simply rejecting your approach.

Welcome getting blown out as great feedback and learn from it. With practice, you will just keep getting better!

As Sinn says in the Love Systems Interview Series on Opening and Transitioning: "Most women are not bitches – they are just bitches to you when you approach them badly. Her bitchy behavior is more of a test than who she actually is."

The faster you fail, the faster you succeed!

If you read the bios of the top guys in Love Systems, the most common story is…failure! The reason that they are now the best in the business is down to their resilience and their willingness to learn from their knocks. For those of us who are not naturally good with women, much of this stuff takes a lot of practice. Because it needs to be instinctive and come over as natural and congruent, no amount of reading books or blogs can achieve this – you need to get out there and use it so that you can truly internalize it.

I got this quote from Mr M and Daxx: ***"You have to fail to succeed, so fail fast"*** – I love this! Once again, welcome the knocks you get with open arms, because these are the experiences that really help you to learn, improve and succeed.

Have no regrets

Imagine you see just one woman each day who you find attractive (a massive underestimate) - over 10 years that would mean 365 days x 10 years = 3650 missed opportunities.

Despite the fact that they are all presumably beautiful (because you found them attractive in the first place), how many hundreds would have met all your personal criteria (smart, funny, loving, etc.) and probably would find you attractive also? Unfortunately you will never know, because you missed them all.

Think about it - does it hurt? It should.

One of Braddock's favorite quotes:

"Failure weighs ounces, regret weighs tons."

You need to filter for women who meet your standards

Your standards should be high, so you should get used to filtering women out. Ballpark - I propose that at least 80% of women you find physically attractive should not meet your standards according to wider criteria, such as personal interests and values, and therefore you need to approach that many more women just so that you increase your chances of identifying which women you really wish to progress things with, not because they respond to your approach, but because they meet your criteria.

Given that you may not be able to set up dates with all of the 20% of women who meet your standards (especially before you've really gotten good at dating), you need to approach even more women just to increase your chances and your experience.

It's difficult to meet women if you don't meet women

This is just a statement of the obvious, but one which hopefully hits home. Many people complain that they don't meet nice women or they cannot find nice women. However, if you are not actually approaching women to introduce yourself in the first place, then you are not exactly helping yourself, are you?

London-based Love Systems Instructor, Keychain, says he lives by what Mahatma Gandhi once said: "You may never know what results come of your action, but if you do nothing there will be no result."

Realize how much power you have

Consider how lucky you are to be a man. As a heterosexual man, you have total power to approach any woman you want — the world is literally your oyster - you have so much choice!

Compare the following:

- **Heterosexual woman:** do you have any idea how incredibly difficult it is for women to cold approach men - the immediate socially-conditioned sub-communication is desperate / easy / low value. By comparison, the sub-communication of a man cold approaching a woman is confidence / strength.

- **Homosexual man:** consider how offended some homo-phobic guys can be when they are hit on by other guys — so much so that they may even get violent or at least verbally aggressive — by comparison women want to be hit on, so the game is completely in your favor.

You have an incredible power and gift that over 50% of the world does not possess. Many guys never take advantage of it. Don't be one of those men that sits around and watches life passing him by. Realize that you have this power and choice and don't waste it!!

Women love to be approached but 95% of men have no approach skill

As you begin approaching women more and more, you will quickly realize that women love to be approached because it flatters and validates their sense of femininity.

Women get approached all the time, but 95% of the time, they are approached badly and this is why they build up an automatic defense shield to fend off guys with no real value – and this is understandable because they just don't have time to deal with every guy who approaches them. But simply by reading this article, you are already ahead of 95% of the male population. Just by being a little different (for example using the openers that you can find in Daytime Dating) and demonstrating confidence, you will see an enormous difference in the way women perceive you.

I do a lot of daytime dating approaches and, when just starting out, I was amazed when my phone number success rate went from around a paltry 10% to around 80% by making just a few tweaks to my approach – but there is no way I could do this unless I took a few knocks in the beginning to get the feedback I needed.

Consider the 8 attraction switches

Let's just remind you of the 8 attraction switches from Daytime Dating – the 8 key male attributes that women are attracted to:

- Appearance
- Confidence
- Humor
- Social Intelligence
- Passion
- Pre-selection
- Status
- Wealth

Do you think that someone with confidence, status, social intelligence, and who is used to being surrounded by and challenging beautiful women, would think twice about approaching a woman he finds attractive?

Obviously not – so neither should you. You need to adopt an air of confidence that sub-communicates that you already have all the attraction switches, until you actually do have them.

Chapter 16: Some Practical Tips to get Going

Fix your inner game!

I was unsure whether to put this as the first or the last practical tip. In fact, I was not even sure if I should include it at all. Why? Because it is not a quick practical tip by any means and the last thing I want is to suggest a tip that is so enormous that it paralyses you into inaction. So here is the condition I attach to this point:

Do not use this as an excuse for not approaching – inner game is a long-term project (that we are / should be all working on all the time) and needs to be done alongside everything else not before (because otherwise none of us would ever make any progress!).

This is a huge topic (in fact the subject of a full-day seminar with Braddock and Mr M) and I won't even pretend to do it justice in just a few lines – so below are just two of my favorite and simplest recommendations. There is some overlap here with "getting in state" (see next point), so you can also do these things before you go out, but for inner game development purposes, try to do these things religiously every day – I suggest the morning (as soon as you get up) and the evening (before you sleep) for just 5-10 minutes each time:

- **Reinforce your successes:** go over any positive interactions with women that you can remember – ideally that day, otherwise recent experiences or simply the most memorable experiences you have. Remind yourself how awesome you are!

- **Visualization:** Imagine that you already possess all the attraction switches. See yourself as the life and soul of the party. See smiling faces, laughter, women being all over you, etc. I often tell clients that it amazes me how women look at me differently now since I developed my dating life – even if I am just walking down the street or sitting in a café in old clothes – don't ask me how, but women can pick up on confidence and find it very attractive – so even if you don't have it yet, just fake it until you make it.

Get in state

This one is really easy. Human beings are extremely state-driven. This is why we teach our clients to be aware of and try to influence a woman's state by keeping your energy high and associating yourself with fun.

You need, therefore, to control your own state first and foremost. Going into a club completely cold can be pretty tough, so you need to get yourself "n the mood and energized before you start your approaches. Here are some of the things I do to get in state:

- Listen to high energy music: listen to whatever works for you. Personally, I like club dance music at high volume.

- One Vodka Red Bull!: I will often drink a can of Red Bull and have a single shot of vodka (I don't drink much in the club, so this is a useful hit before I go out. The Red Bull gives me energy for the entire evening and the vodka shot triggers memories of fun times out with friends.)

- Grinning: studies have shown that the simple act of smiling triggers the brain to release serotonin which elevates mood. Grin like an idiot for 5 minutes – guaranteed to put you in a good mood and gives you that positive energy that women find infectious!

- Subtext: similar to visualization, a tip from Love Systems Instructor, Cajun, is an acting technique called "subtext" (http://www.lovesystems.com/publications/subtext) simply approach under the (unspoken) "subtext" that you have already slept with the woman before you begin talking with her. You may also want to repeat a sentence or two to that effect, e.g. "I like you, you like me, you cannot get enough of me because I fuck like a rock star and we always have loads of fun together." Believe it is true and you will sub-communicate confidence and an air of abundance.

Be consistent – find your window!

The more you practice, the less anxiety you will feel. So make sure you make time to practice. UK-based Love Systems Instructor, Keychain, refers to this as "Finding your window," i.e. identify what part of your day or week you can consistently use to practice your approaches. For him, it was his commute to and from work on the train. A friend in New York uses his lunch break every day. Whatever works for you – identify your window and make it part of your daily or weekly schedule.

Get a wingman

The reasons why a wingman is so important are:

- You will push each other into going out and into conversations that you might shy away from on your own.

- You can give each other feedback that is not always obvious to yourself.

- You can reward each other when approaches go well. Little things like high fives and (masculine!) hugs are great for associating positive emotions with approaches.

- You can set tough goals for each other with financial pain: a popular wingman game is to hand $200 to your wing and tell him to give you back $20 for every approach you make.

Set realistic goals

You need to set yourself goals that suit the stage of your learning process. The last thing you want to do is to set unrealistic goals that just demoralize you and make you associate the process with pain.

If you are just starting out and still find approaching terrifying then don't expect to get laid off each approach. Instead congratulate yourself on pushing your (current) boundaries, even if it is just talking to women e.g. just asking them for directions or asking for the time.

However, it is a fine balance between constant repetition to establish comfort and trying to push your boundaries...if in doubt...push your boundaries! If there is one consistent error that guys make, it is in underestimating what they are capable of or what a woman is willing to do with them. Wherever you believe the line to be, it is always much further than you think!

Sticks and carrots

Your goal should be to associate pleasure with approaching and pain with any failure to approach:

- **Sticks / Punishments:** London-based Love Systems Instructor, Vercetti, uses an elastic band around his wrist as a tool for punishment. Whenever he fails to approach, he snaps the elastic band to associate pain with failure to approach. You should use whatever works for you, e.g. skip TV for an evening or your regular beer after work.

- **Carrots / Rewards:** your personal reward could be as simple as a self-congratulation (I say to myself quietly "yes, yes – awesome job, Carbeau", smile, clench my fist and really savor the moment) or you could buy yourself a smoothie, café latte or whatever else works for you.

I recommend you set yourself specific goals attached to specific rewards / punishments. In the beginning especially, you should aim for multiple approaches to really break the camel's back. So, for example, you could go out with the goal of doing 10 approaches before you can go home.

Keep a success journal

I keep emphasizing how important it is for you to associate approaching with positive emotions – when you think of approaching, you should get excited, not fearful.

But you often forget how many great approaches you have done, especially if you have more rejection than successful approaches, which is perfectly normal as you start out. But you will surprise yourself - if you think hard enough – when you realize how many great approaches you have actually done.

So one of the tricks you should employ is to keep a journal of positive experiences. Don't worry about the fact that it is kind of cheating – because when you flick back through your entries, they are guaranteed to energize you and make you want to jump straight back in field!

The 3-second rule

This is an old classic and every bit as valuable as it has always been. The rule states that you need to approach a woman within 3 seconds of seeing her. There are a couple of reasons why this is important:

a. The longer you wait, the harder it actually becomes to approach because your brain creates so many reasons for not approaching (she is with someone, she looks busy / in a hurry, etc.). I suggest you establish a standard opener (or no more than 2-3) and become very comfortable delivering it without even thinking – that way, you can move immediately and not let your pussy brain sabotage you.

b. If you react quickly, your attractiveness to the woman increases exponentially. Because of this, you actually have a lot less work to do to build attraction later. It pays huge dividends and makes the rest of your interaction much easier, believe me. A few months back, a Spanish girl entered a bar in Philadelphia and I reached out with my arm almost instantly, stopping her in her tracks, and delivered my standard direct opener. She looked at me with gooey eyes that just oozed attraction and said "wow – that was fast!"

Implement the 3-second rule immediately – it will turbo-charge your dating life!

Short-setting:

- **Night-time approaches:** Short-setting is a low risk warm-up routine that we teach to clients where you move around the club / bar interacting with other punters in short 20-30sec conversations. You should have no agenda (say things like "how's it going?" or just high five them) so it is pretty much impossible to get rejected. It also builds huge social proof since women will notice you interacting with lots of people and wonder who you are (the goal should be to look like you literally own the place).

- **Daytime approaches:** Short-setting does not really apply to daytime dating since there are not a set number of people in a single location (as in a club/bar) and the environment is not appropriate for strangers to walk up to each other asking how they are and asking for high fives - people will just think you are weird! However, if you are having trouble making your first approach, try just walking up to beautiful women and asking them what time it is or ask for directions to a specific nearby landmark.

10. Implement Savoy's 20% Rule

One of the things that holds people back is fear of the unknown, i.e. what happens if she tells me to get lost? What happens if I forget what to say, etc. Savoy has a "20% rule" which states that, whenever you feel like you have reached the end of your conversation (i.e. you think you have nothing to say or that you are getting nowhere), you must force yourself to stay in for 20% longer!

- Experience it, get over it: The best way to get over fear is to face it. Once you experience it, you usually realize that it's actually not that bad.

- 20% longer in conversation forces you to try new stuff: You often find that you surprise yourself with how much more you can achieve just by giving it a little longer and, even if you get rejected, you will have tried new stuff you don't normally use and can therefore also learn what works and what doesn't.

- 20% longer in field forces you to try tougher groups of women: try to stay in the club or on the street 20% longer than the point at which you want to go home. It may just be that you have only approach the easy groups, but try the mixed groups or the seated groups. It may surprise you what you can do. The difference between a good night and a bad night is almost always more conversations. You never regret doing more, only doing less!

I had a client recently who had an irrational fear of getting thrown out of clubs for approaching women. I tried to throw him into conversations with openers that would push him beyond his comfort zone and make him realize this was highly unlikely to happen. On one approach, he hit on a woman just as her boyfriend came up behind her, but the boyfriend just stood there and waited for my client and his girlfriend to finish their conversation. This experience alone proved to him that you can push things much further than you think and blew away all his fears about getting thrown out of clubs.

If you really want to push yourself, an extension of the 20% rule is the *"there's no way out rule"* where you don't allow yourself to eject until she either walks off or until you have her phone number / go home with her. This is sometimes affectionately known as the *"blow me or blow me out rule."*

Push yourself out of your comfort zone – it builds serious approach muscle!

Conclusion

Print these out and stick them on your bathroom mirror so you see them every day.

- Approach anxiety is natural and good!

- Fear through "living on the edge" is intrinsically masculine and should be sought out, not avoided - "re-program" yourself so that you associate approaching women with fun.

- Take Action! "As long as nothing happens, nothing ever will"

- Enjoy the dopamine hit when you approach and form the APPROACH HABIT.

- Nobody can reject you based on a cold approach (she can only reject your approach, not you).

- The faster you fail, the faster you succeed!

- "Failure weighs ounces, regret weighs tons."

- Realize the power you possess to APPROACH ANYBODY YOU CHOOSE.

- You need to approach more women so you can filter for quality.

- Be the attraction switches – think: Status, Confidence, Pre-selection, Passion – act like it is you until it actually becomes you.

- Work on your inner game. Women can smell if you are congruent.

- Get in state: music, physiognomy, visualization, sub-texting, incantations/mind scripts.

- Find your window.

- Get a wingman.

- Set realistic but stretch goals and reward/punish yourself for good/bad behavior.

- Short-set.

- Keep a success journal.

- Apply the 3-second rule.

- Have 1-3 standard openers that you can roll out without thinking.

- Apply the 20% rule / or the "blow me or blow me out" rule.

- HAVE FUN!!!!

Carbeau

Chapter 17: Master Your Dating Life in One Year

Introduction by Joshua Farmer

Learning dating science is a huge task that is made no easier by the vast amounts of information out there. The purpose of this article is to make sure that you learn dating science the right way and to help you learn it in record time.

Guys find learning dating science so difficult because it incorporates a lot of different aspects of learning. In some ways it is like learning a new language – you have to learn a new way of communicating and new things to say, along with new vocal tones and rhythms of your speech. In other ways it is like learning a new sport – you have to correct your body language, the way you move and you have to practice progressing physically. There are also mental aspects to learning – you need to overcome fear and social awkwardness, become confident and learn to deal with rejection.

It is the same as trying to learn Spanish while being on a court learning tennis. It cannot be done if you do too many things at once.

There are so many discrete aspects that engage different resources that most guys feel overwhelmed by the amount of things they have to learn. Couple this with the anxiety of mastering an area of life that is so important and essential, and it is a recipe for frustration.

It can seem difficult to practice and to get good in a reasonably short amount of time. A lot guys take five or six years to master being good with women, a lot more just don't make it. If you follow the advice in this article, you will have the tools to learn to be successful with women within one year, if you practice hard and smart.

To practice smart you need to utilize some rules of productivity that have helped in all areas of my life, and allowed me to improve my dating life in a relatively short space of time. It's not that I am particularly clever or good at learning new things, in fact I probably spent the same amount of cumulative time practicing dating science as every other Love

Systems coach. It's just that I learned to ignore the stuff that didn't matter and the stuff that didn't help me to improve. I packed the same learning into a shorter period of real time.

Follow these simple rules, and your dating life will skyrocket in an unbelievable amount of time. It will be hard, but the things worth doing in life always are.

Joshua Farmer

The Pareto Principle

An old Italian economist, Vilfredo Pareto, discovered in 1906 that 80% of the country's wealth lay in the hands of only 20% of the inhabitants. Delving deeper into this discovery, he found that the ratio of 80/20 formed the basis for a lot of other things, like 80% of the vegetables in his garden grew from only 20% of the seeds.

His discovery is now a recognized principle in business, sales and economics. The premise is that 80% of all outputs come from only 20% of the inputs. For instance, in sales, it is a given fact that 80% of your revenue will come from only 20% of your customers. The ratio may be more like 90/10, but 80/20 is the average.

Thinking about this in terms of productivity, you can use this to your advantage. Taking the sales example, if you identify who the 20% of your customers are, you can literally ignore the other 80% of your customers and still generate 80% of your revenue. This frees up 80% of your time to focus on other things, like identifying and attracting more customers similar to the base 20%.

Say only 20 of your customers out of 100 generate 80 million dollars, you can 'fire' the other 80 customers and lose out on 20 million dollars – but find another 20 customers similar to the first 20 and you now have 160 million dollars in revenue from only 40 customers, rather than 100 million from 100 customers. This is a huge timesaver.

I used this concept in my marathon training. I was spending 6 days a week training for up to 4 hours a day, running myself into the ground and leaving me hardly any time for anything else. So I looked at 20 of the best marathon training schedules and researched sports nutrition and physiology to identify what they all had in common. I found that there were only 3 key, essential ingredients to marathon training – long runs, tempo runs and speed work. In other words, 20% of the ingredients of a training plan lead to 80% of the improvements.

I did one workout pertaining to each of these ingredients on each of my training days. My training schedule dropped to 3 days a week, and my total hours to an average of 3 a week. The amazing thing was, my times improved by a huge margin.

By ignoring the extra useless training aspects which were wasting my time and energy and focussing on the key ingredients, I was able to free up a huge amount of time, and still improve my times significantly.

How does this relate to dating science?

If you identify the key aspects of dating science (20%), which lead to the most improvements (80%), you will improve your dating science significantly in a shorter space of time than the guy who is trying to do everything at once.

Luckily, you don't have to identify them yourselves. I am going to give you the essential key ingredients that you must focus on to improve your dating science exponentially. You can ignore the rest.

The 80/20 of dating science

Approach Approach Approach!

You've heard it countless times and you'll hear it countless more: just approaching women is by far the best way to improve your dating science by 1000%. A lot of the questions you have about dating science can be solved instantly by just going out, approaching a lot, failing, trying again and figuring out what works for you. You cannot get good if you don't approach a lot and approach often – exercise that approach muscle at least once a day to keep it strong.

Niels Bohr, famous physicist, once said that an expert is simply a person who has made all of the mistakes possible in a limited field. I agree. I got good at dating by approaching a lot and making all of the mistakes there are to be made. You cannot learn unless you fail – so get used to failing. This article will help you fail fast.

Body Language

Body language is such a huge part of dating science and an aspect that guys tend to ignore. Dating science is not just about routines and what to say. I would even go so far as to say that improving your body language accounts for 80 – 90% of the improvements in a guy's dating science.

Every Bootcamp we have clients with bad body language who try to open with lines and routines and get blown out. When we work with them to fix these bad habits of posture and movement, they start opening consistently using the exact same lines.

Good body language conveys so much about yourself to a woman that you cannot express verbally. How you carry yourself conveys to people the sum total of everything you are. It improves your first impression (what Malcolm Gladwell calls your "thin slice") – women have a very good ability to sum up a guy in a fraction of a second. She will assess your body language and think back to all of the guys in her life who have exhibited the same trait. She will then project the traits of those people onto you, whether you have them or not. If you have good body language, she will think you are also confident, wealthy and good with women. Have bad body language and she will think you are weak, nervous and shy.

Progression

I see it all the time. A client is confident and witty. He approaches well every single time and gets the woman laughing and flirting. She's attracted. But he doesn't get a phone number, he doesn't get a date, he doesn't go home with her. He gets nothing. Why?

He doesn't progress. In terms of the Love Systems Triad he doesn't progress either emotionally, logistically or physically. You need to keep progressing otherwise you're moving backwards. If approaching takes balls, then progressing along any of the 3 ladders takes more balls. It can be a good feeling to be able to approach, transition and attract a woman to the point where she's eating out of your hand, but if you're going home at night with nothing to show for it, then there is a problem. You need to step up and progress things.

Emotionally, this means not getting stuck in Attraction. Women need to be guided through a range of emotions, namely Attraction, Qualification,

Comfort and Seduction. If they experience one emotion for too long they get bored and switch off.

Ever been talking to a woman and she's having fun, flirting and laughing, then all of a sudden she gets cold and won't answer simple questions, or simply grabs her friends to go dancing? You didn't guide her to a new emotion and she got bored. You're now the guy who hasn't got the balls to progress things further with her, and her attraction for you is dead.

In a conversation, always be moving forward in emotional progression. Your aim should be to get to Comfort in all of your approaches. As Attraction can happen pretty quickly, you should be getting to Qualification as soon as possible, and Comfort soon after.

Logistically, you absolutely need to move her. This means either moving her around the bar, moving her to the side of the street, taking her to get ice cream around the corner or even taking her home. Isolation is a big part of this step and is essential in a night environment.

Progressing logistically during the night can also simply mean turning her around, or moving her a few feet from her friends. During the day it can be as simple as telling her to move to the side of the street to get out of the way of the crowd. Talking to her in different locations, however small, creates more Comfort because people trust each other more if they've been to different places together in a short space of time.

The one logistical thing that can improve your dating science drastically is asking for her phone number. It sounds simple, but it is a huge step that a lot of guys cannot take. Practice progressing logistically, asking for the phone number, in every conversation you get into, even if you know she won't give it you. Do this, and when it's time to ask when she's really into you, you won't get scared and you'll just ask.

Physical progression is something that a lot of guys have a problem with. But if you want to sleep with a woman it is absolutely necessary. A woman needs to be comfortable with your touch before you seduce and sleep with her.

Physical progression is done in small steps and needs to be gauged according to her comfort level. If you go out and just practice progressing physically, strong and fast, every time you go out, your dating science will improve tenfold. You will learn that you can push physical progression further than you thought possible.

The importance of physical progression is not to be ignored – if you go through all of the same progression steps (logistical and emotional) but you don't progress physically, you will be unceremoniously put in the Friend Zone. No one wants that.

Visualization

Visualization is a very important part of learning anything. It is a huge topic, but the basics of it will help you a huge deal. The basic premise is that your mind cannot tell the difference between imagined stimuli and real stimuli. Your mind produces the exact same physiological responses to anything you imagine in the same way it would react to the same thing in real life.

To experience this, close your eyes and imagine yourself having sex with a woman you find extremely hot. Really try to feel everything and experience everything in your mind. Your heart will start to race and you will feel aroused. Your brain is creating the same physiological responses it would do if you were actually having sex.

This is a very useful tool. It can be used to rehearse things that have never happened to you. Imagine yourself giving a speech to 1000 people. At first you will feel nervous, even though you are only sitting in your living room. If you now start to imagine people smiling and clapping, and start to imagine saying the exact things you want to say, you will feel less nervous. Rehearse this 20 times in your head. When it comes time to give the speech in real life, your body and mind **will think that it has already done this 20 times** and it will not be as nervous.

Visualization can also be used to correct things that went wrong. Remember a time when you got blown out by a woman or you ran out of things to say or do. Now close your eyes and imagine yourself back in this moment in time, talking to this woman. Really feel it. You'll feel nervous again. Now run the interaction in your mind, **but imaginatively come up with things to say and things to do to correct your previous mistakes.** Do this over and over again until you can run that conversation from start to finish, saying and doing the things that you want to do. When it comes time to do this for real, your mind will think it has already done it and it will come up with these things automatically.

As a pianist, mental rehearsal was a very important aspect of my training. I would take an hour out of my day and close my eyes, and run through a piece in my head until I could literally see myself playing each key the way it was supposed to be played, in the correct order. This would make sure that I knew exactly how to play the piece, rather than relying on muscle memory in my fingers. While I was doing this, my mind was telling the muscles in my fingers to make miniscule movements **as if I was actually playing the piano.** When it came time to actually play, my fingers though they had done this 100 times before. It is a way to rehearse anything, wherever you are.

If you still don't believe me, tie a shoelace around a pencil and let it hang down in front of you, keeping your arm straight. Now don't move a muscle, but imagine the pencil making a circular movement. Really imagine it. It will start to move in a circular motion. Your brain is telling your arm to perform tiny movements according to the instructions you are giving it. The more it starts to move, the bigger the movements your brain will tell your arm. For those interested, this is how a Ouija Board works...

For dating science, it is important to visualize your approaches and anything else that you wish to correct. Run through interactions 50 times to make sure that you know exactly what you want to say and do. When it comes time to do it in real life, this mental rehearsal will mean that you will be able to perform these actions with no problems at all.

Get a Wingman

A wingman is useful for so many reasons, amongst the most important are: you have fun together in the club and on the streets, he wings you to distract her friends so you can isolate her, you look social in the club with someone to talk to and you both push each other to approach.

Learning on your own can be educational, but the point of this article is to teach you how to learn to have great dating ability in a very short space of time. Getting a wingman is an essential part of this process.

Keep a Diary

This is related to the point about goal setting which comes later. Keeping an approach journal, where you write down all your approaches every day, will keep you on track when you start to falter. It is essential to constantly recognise a) where your common sticking points are and b) how far you have come. If at any time you feel like you're not progressing, look through the journal and you'll instantly see how far you've come.

Routines

Even though body language rates much higher on the scale of productivity, there is no better way to skyrocket your dating science in the beginning that memorizing some routines. These are the exact things that I and the other coaches say whenever we meet women. Sometimes guys want to start off by just being themselves and making up their own things to say. To this I say, it hasn't been working for you up until now so something needs to change.

One of the first things a client usually asks me is "What do I say to a woman to make her like me" or "Look at that woman over there, what do I say?" This kind of thing cannot go through your mind when you see a woman – you need to move your feet and approach within 3 seconds. You need to know exactly what you are going to say. Memorizing routines frees up your mental space to concentrate on things like body language and logistics. Use them as training wheels while you learn to be social and attract women, and after a while you'll find that you start saying your own things anyway.

You need to free up your mind to concentrate on progressing the interaction. If you have some routines cued up already you will be able to effortlessly move from Attraction to Qualification without thinking.

Bootcamps and Workshops

Finally, if you really want to learn in the shortest timeframe possible, taking a Love Systems Bootcamp or Workshop is by far the best way to shortcut your journey. It can take years off someone's learning curve. You get to see and hear first-hand how approaches should look, how lines should be delivered, and how confident guys stand and move.

In terms of sports psychology, beginning sportsmen learn quickest when they watch an action being performed repeatedly, and then they go and try the same action themselves. Our minds and bodies are connected so intricately that when your mind sees something being performed, it is able to direct your body to do the exact same movement (and with sports actions, sometimes 1000 different muscle contractions) perfectly.

Selective ignorance

On our journey into productivity an essential part is learning to ignore a lot of information you don't need. In all walks of life and business, people waste a lot of time reading information that they either cannot use immediately or confuses them to the point of being unable to take action.

In terms of learning dating science, this means that the vast majority of guys spend their time reading more information on every aspect of dating science than they could ever use. Their heads get so filled with tonnes of routines, ways to deal with shit tests, how to deal with obstacles, a new way to transition or more openers. When they eventually get out into a nightclub (assuming they get that far) their heads are filled with knowledge that they are prevented from doing anything for fear of not remembering everything.

This next sentence, if adhered to, will change your life and will drastically improve your learning curve. Ready? **Only read something if it is immediately actionable and/or solves a problem you are currently experiencing.**

You could spend a lifetime reading every single bit of material you can find on dating science, but if you can't actually go out and use that information immediately, everything you just read was a waste of your time. All that will happen is that you will re-read the same information later on down the line when it is relevant to you.

Here are some tips that will increase your productivity by 500%:

- Use The Attraction Forums and other dating related forums retrospectively. This means that it is far better, and quicker in terms of learning, to go out and approach a lot of women in one night. Take one opener, one transition and one attraction routine and go out and use them one by one. Make a note of all the problems that you run into while doing this. Then, when you get back that night, or the next morning, read only the information on the dating forums that specifically deals with the problems you had. And also, only read that information if it is something that you can actually use and implement the next night. **Read nothing else.** Now go out again and use this information to solve those problems.

- Only read information and advice posted on the forums if it is posted by an Instructor or a respected member of the community. Reading and remembering/trying to use information given by anyone else is like asking a guy on the street how to perform brain surgery. A lot of these guys writing 'advice' have never slept with a woman, let alone approached one. Seek out the best information by the guys who have been there, done that and solved the same problems. It might be fun to get into a heated debate about which semi-direct opener is the best, but it won't help you progress in the slightest. Ignore the keyboard jockeys, and don't be one yourself.

- Focus on one thing at a time. Ignore the rest for the time being. If you are having problems with Transitioning, there is no point reading about how to solve Comfort issues. Read quality information about Transitioning, and then go out and use this information repeatedly until you can transition like a pro.

- Conversely, only read something if it something you are having a problem with. If you can open and transition, but your problem is Attraction, then why would you read about new ways to open or transition? Focus on the things that solve your problems, and nothing else.

Parkinson's law

Have you ever wasted a 9-5 day doing one or two things, then the next day you have a doctor's appointment so you need to complete a day's work in 2 hours, and miraculously you can? This is Parkinson's Law at work.

If you give someone a time limit to complete a task, they will tend to use every single bit of this time to complete it. So give someone 8 hours in a working day to complete some tasks, and they will complete them in 8 hours. Give that same person only 1 hour to complete the same tasks, and they will be able to complete them in 1 hour.

Giving myself extremely short time limits is something I have been doing for years, even before I started researching productivity. At university, I would ignore the 2 week deadline for an essay, and instead give myself one day to complete it. I would literally sit in the library from 9am to 5am the next day and just get on with it. Then I would party and enjoy university life for the next 13 days while everyone else was stressing about their essay. It's a secret which made me look like a genius, seemingly not working at all, while producing 1st class work. I'm not a genius, I just learnt to ignore interruptions and time wasting and pack everything essential that I needed to do in a really short timeframe. Other people simply chose to do the same amount of work, but spaced out over 2 weeks.

This relates to dating science in many ways, but the most important is to use Parkinson's Law when you are out at night or approaching women on the streets during the day. If you go out to a bar or a club at 10pm, knowing that you are staying there for 4 or 5 hours until it closes, I guarantee you that you will use all of this time to open maybe 5 or 6 women. If, however, you go out and set yourself 1 hour to complete 6 approaches, I bet that you will complete this task no problem. The rest of your time can then be spent on reflecting on your problems, correcting them by approaching more, or by re-opening women from before. Use this technique if you routinely stand around at the bar or the dance floor for 2 hours before approaching.

This is especially relevant during daytime dating. At first, I wasted 8 or 9 hours traipsing the streets of London every Saturday and Sunday waiting for the perfect approach and I would approach maybe 3 or 4 sets. This is not productive and I wasn't learning very fast at all. When I started going out and giving myself 2 hours to approach 10 women, my learning curve shot up rapidly. You don't want to put aside your life for a year by daytime dating all day every weekend. You can get the same amount of experience in 2 hours that you can get in 10 hours if you use the time wisely.

Goal setting

It's all very well knowing how to be productive, but if you don't know where you're going, then you'll waste time flapping about with no direction.

The human mind is goal orientated. We need long term and short term goals to work towards. Our minds are like homing missiles – we give it a goal and we set it moving, and during this time it moves forward, corrects course when it makes a mistake and eventually hits the target.

In terms of dating science, before you go out to the clubs or hit the streets, you need to know:

   a. What you are going to work on that day

   b. What your goal is for the week

   c. What your goal is for the month

   d. What your goal is for every other month

e. What your 6-month goal is

f. What your 1 year goal is

You need to write these down and stick to them so that you know where you are going. Write them in a journal, and every time you achieve a goal write it down in that journal. If at any time you feel like you are not progressing, then you can look back in your journal and see how far you have improved since the beginning. Lots and lots of baby steps add up to a huge stride forward in improvement.

For example, your goal after 1 year might be to be able to consistently date women you meet on the street. This is a huge goal that cannot be accomplished unless you break it down into smaller goals and steps.

So your 6-month goal, using the above end goal, might be to consistently get phone numbers from women you approach on the street. Now break this 6 months down into 6 goals that you want to accomplish every month, working backwards from month 6:

Month 6 – Consistently get phone numbers

Month 5 – Consistently be able to move her logistically

Month 4 – Consistently be able to prolong the interaction and qualify

Month 3 – Consistently be able to convey attraction triggers

Month 2 – Consistently be able to transition

Month 1 – Consistently be able to approach and get her to stop walking

This is a sample and your actual goals will be different depending on your skill level and where you want to be in 1 year. Now you need to quantify these goals. Take the first month, month 1, and create 4 quantifiable goals that you can easily achieve:

Week 4 – Approach 20 women anywhere

Week 3 – Approach 20 women who are walking

Week 2 – Approach 20 women who are sitting down

Week 1 – Approach 20 women who are standing around

20 women a week is entirely doable. Taking small baby steps like this, you will have approached 1040 women by the end of the year. Again, this is just an example – your quantifiable goals will be different. You might want to quantify teases for night time approaches– this week I want to use X tease 10 times in conversations etc. But always remember to work backwards from your goals, this way you will always have the end goal in mind.

You must make sure that these goals are attainable. If you set goals that are too hard to hit, you will become discouraged. You need to set goals that you can hit, so that when you hit them you get a positive reference experience of reaching that goal. This puts you in a positive frame of mind. Positive reference experiences reinforce the belief that you can achieve goals that you set, and the snowball effect is that with each goal you reach, the positive reference experiences accumulate to create a very positive self image.

It is inevitable that your goals will change once you get going. This is okay. Reassess your goals once every week to see if you are still on track. If you are, great. If not, identify what's holding you back and reassess your timeline. I guarantee that if you follow the advice in this article, you will most likely be approaching more women than your target number and be learning at an increased rate.

Finally, break the first week down into the number of times you are going to go out, and work on one aspect of dating science at a time. For example, if you are going to go out 3 times, on Thursday, Friday and Saturday, you need to know what you are going to do on these 3 days. If your first week goal is to approach 10 women using a direct opener, concentrate on that and that only **until you can do it without problems**. Then you can start to work on something else. In other words, choose **one** direct opener, ignore everything else, and use it to approach your target number that day.

A sample training plan for a week of night time approaching

So how do we use all of the above information to form a coherent progression model to learn dating science the right way and to learn it fast? You need a training plan, like any other sport, language learning or musical instrument.

You need to plan your week so that it includes your goals and so that you make sure you are concentrating on including only the 80/20 aspects of dating science.

Thursday:

In the club:

GOAL – Approach 10 women using a direct opener

SELECTIVE IGNORANCE – choose one direct opener and ignore everything else

PARKINSON'S LAW – do my approaches in 2 hours

80/20 – concentrating here on Approaching

At home afterwards or the morning after:

SELECTIVE IGNORANCE – identify the problems you encountered during your approaches and read only the information that will directly solve it and will be immediately actionable.

Ignore everything else.

VISUALIZATION – run through all 10 conversations in your mind and identify where you went wrong; re-run the interaction in your mind and use the information you just read to plug the holes until you can run the perfect conversation in your head, putting right the problems you encountered.

Friday:

In the club:

GOAL – Approach 10 women using a direct opener

SELECTIVE IGNORANCE – choose one direct opener and ignore everything else

PARKINSON'S LAW – do my approaches in 2 hours

80/20 – today concentrate on progression

At home afterwards or the morning after:

SELECTIVE IGNORANCE – same as Thursday

VISUALIZATION – same as Thursday

Saturday:

In the club:

GOAL – Approach 10 women using a direct opener, and transition in the majority of approaches

SELECTIVE IGNORANCE – choose one direct opener and one transition and ignore everything else

PARKINSON'S LAW – do my approaches in 2 hours

80/20 – today concentrate on body language

At home afterwards or the morning after:

SELECTIVE IGNORANCE – same as Thursday

VISUALIZATION – same as Thursday

You can see here that there is a very small progression – you add Transitioning on Saturday. You can also see that you are concentrating on different things each day – Approaching, progressing and body language. After a weekend like this, you should already be improving 200% in a short space of time.

Appendix

Glossary

Approaching – Initiating a conversation with a woman or group of women. Also known as opening or starting a conversation.

Bootcamp – An official Love Systems training program consisting of a weekend spent with a cadre of international renowned dating coaches, which teaches you ultimate confidence and competence in talking to and seducing attractive women.

Close – Taking a phone number, kissing or sleeping with a woman.

Cold approach – Approaching a woman or group of women you don't know. The opposite of a warm approach which is an approach where you have already have some connection to the woman through your social circle.

Congruence – Consistency of behavior with the identity you portray. If you display a particularly personality trait (for example, integrity), congruence requires that you act in a manner consistent for someone that has that trait.

Day Game (Daytime Dating) – The practice of meeting women during the daytime.

Escalate – To progress an interaction with a woman further. Usually refers to physical or logistical progression, but can also refer to emotional progession.

Frame – The context or subtext of an interaction. You can set frames to interactions by the manner in which you act, what you say and how you say it. For example, teasing a woman you just met sets the frame that you are comfortable and confident in yourself.

Game – A term for the process of meeting and seducing women. Often used to refer to the book, The Game, by Neil Strauss.

Opening – Initiating a conversation with a woman or group of women. Also known as approaching or starting a conversation.

Pick up – A slang term for meeting and seducing women.

Routine – A line or pre-written script designed to elicit a specific response from a woman or to continue a conversation with her.

Routines can be helpful when you have absolutely no idea what to say to a woman in order to develop fundamental values, for example confidence, in your interactions.

Triad Model – A systematic model for interacting with women in a way that is attractive, based on three strands: emotional, physical and logistical progression.

Value – What makes someone or something desirable.

Resources

This book is a great tool, and will provide you with a strong foundation for improving your skills and bolstering your confidence with women. With the knowledge gleaned from these pages and lots of practice, you will see a marked improvement in your interactions with women.

However, not everything can be taught in one book. Some techniques are hard to convey on the written page, and others are far too advanced for general consumption. For that reason, we've compiled a list of further resources that can help you achieve even more.

In general, these are the things you should be considering for improving your skills after reading this book:

1. An Overall System
2. Routines – a Foundation
3. 21st Century Pickup – Text and Phone Game
4. Workshops and Training
5. Advanced Material
6. Keep up to Date

An overall system – Magic Bullets

The systems and techniques in this book were designed to be used with Magic Bullets as the foundation. Most of you have probably read Magic Bullets, but if you haven't, head over to the Magic Bullets page (http://LoveSystems.com/Magic-Bullets) and pick it up (or download the free chapters).

Magic Bullets is the quintessential guide to dating science today, and is the Love Systems "bible." It's also a living book, in that we are constantly experimenting and pushing the frontiers of knowledge, and new discoveries get added to future versions of the book. If you bought a legal copy of the book, these updated versions are sent to you, for free, automatically.

Routines – a foundation

Magic Bullets provides the framework for the entire Love Systems structure, and is the first step in mastering dating science. Learning advanced routines and tactics for every step of the interaction is the second step. While many of you are probably already familiar with the Love Systems Routines Manual Volume 1, some may have missed it.

The Love Systems Routines Manual Volume 1 is a comprehensive guide to learning and mastering the use of routines. It not only explains how and why routines work, but also provides a compilation of hundreds of the very best and most effective openers, conversation starters, and routines from all of the top talent in the world of dating science including Savoy, The Don, Fader, Mr. M, Sheriff, Braddock, Sinn, IN10SE, Tyler Durden, and more.

If you want access to 200 pages of what has been called the most practical and immediately useful information on seduciton avaliable anywhere, or you just need a refresher on the basics of routines, how to use them, and how to create your own, then **check out the Love Systems Routines Manual Volume 1 here (or download the free chapters):**

http://www.lovesystems.com/Routines-Manual

Love Systems was also proud to release the follow up book, Routines Manual Volume 2. Stuffed with hundreds more advanced routines and techniques that you can use right now, with this volume you will never run out of things to say. Volume 2 also includes bonus chapters on Cold Reads, Palm Reading, and much, much more. Check it out, along with free chapters you can download right now, here:

http://www.lovesystems.com/Routines-Manual-2

21st century pickup – text and phone game

To put it simply, if you don't have rock solid text and phone game these days, you're in trouble. Women (and men too) communicate more than ever via mobile devices, and your game has to adjust accordingly. Thankfully, two of Love Systems' most experienced instructors have put together the number one product on the subject. Braddock and Mr. M's Ultimate Guide to Text and Phone Game teaches you the basics and provides you with dozens of scripts that you can adapt to your life for guaranteed successful text and phone game. Check it out here:

Workshops and training

You can read about it, see it, and hear it, but there's really no substitute for actually doing it.

Live training usually involves three things:

1. Intensive classroom seminars, with individualized feedback on your fashion, identity, routines, and rigorous drills and exercises to practice opening and approaching, storytelling, qualification, and so on. You will be prepared and ready to succeed from the first night.

2. Approaching and attempting to seduce random beautiful women, over and over, anywhere from coffee shops to bars. A professional dating coach will watch and listen and tell you after each approach what you did right and wrong and how to improve for the next one. And you'll keep doing it until you improve.

3. Watching and listening to a master dating coach at work, as he demonstrates various techniques and gives you behaviors and strategies to model. You can see how a master dating coach can attract even the most unapproachable women - live. This is important. If you don't know what solid game really looks like, it's very hard to develop it for yourself.

The Love Systems bootcamp (www.lovesystems.com/Bootcamps) include 3 days of seminar work, 2 nights of field work (where you and the instructors go out to meet and practice on beautiful women), and a money-back guarantee. The Love Systems Day Game Workshop (www..lovesystems.com/Daygame) includes 8 hours of seminar work, 8 hours of field work, and the same money-back guarantee. The authors of this book, and many of the contributors to it, are Love Systems instructors. These are the top dating coaches and workshops available today.

Love Systems also offers individualized or one-on-one training (www.lovesystems.com/individualized). This is more expensive, but may be more convenient for some people.

It's easy to postpone attending a workshop. They're not cheap and they're not always convenient. We can say with confidence that this is a mistake. Both of us are former workshop students, as are virtually all Love Systems instructors. On your first day of the workshop, you will probably be blown away by the instructors' skills. Don't be. They were once in your chair. If you learn from them and practice what you've learned, your skills can equal or exceed theirs. We've seen this happen over and over; that's how we recruit new instructors.

There's never a perfect time to take a workshop. There's always a reason not to. Part of dating science is internal transformation, and that includes seizing the moment. If you're serious about having beautiful women as a normal and easy part of your life, then make it happen. Now. Waiting a year just means that you will have one year less to enjoy your new skills once you develop them. You don't get extra time at the end to enjoy your life just because you were late getting started.

Another pitfall some people fall into is waiting to take a workshop until their skills improve. This is backward. The progress people make after a workshop is infinitely quicker than the progress they made before one. And you should have the results you want now, or in a few months, as opposed to some distant future point.

If you've read this book and Magic Bullets, start planning your workshop now. Pick a date. Sign up. Pay your deposit. Make it happen for real.

Selected advanced material

By far the best source of advanced material is a monthly audio program creatively known as the Interview Series. Every month, two of the world's top dating coaches are interviewed together on a specific subject, ranging from Approaching to Seduction or from Phone Game to Threesomes. It's a unique product, since every topic gets treated in tremendous depth, from at least two perspectives, and there's an opportunity to hear the tonality and delivery that the masters use in different situations.

We strongly recommend subscribing to the interview series at (http://www.lovesystems.com/ivs). It's $24.99 per month.

When you subscribe, you will be sent the current month's interview, and a new interview every month afterward. So you don't have to start back at Vol. 1, but all of the previous interviews do make an excellent home study library for an amazing number of different topics.

That being said, it's much cheaper to subscribe (about 50% off). Plus subscribers get the interviews slightly before everyone else, and other goodies including their own mailing list and bonus content.

Other than getting Magic Bullets, **this is the single most important thing you can do right now:**

http://www.lovesystems.com/ivs

Advanced material, by topic

In this section, we've also combined all of these previous interviews with some other resources we recommend, and sorted them by topic. For anything you are having trouble with or want to improve, you can go straight to the source.

Learning Game:

Mr. M and Rokker on The Right Way to Learn Game

http://www.lovesystems.com/cd17

Braddock, Rokker, and Mr. M on Sticking Points
http://lovesystems.com/cd27

Approaching and Bridgeing:

Sinn and Savoy on Opening
http://www.LoveSystems.com/cd1

The Don and Tenmagnet on The First Five Minutes
http://lovesystems.com/cd14

Attraction:

Future and Tenmagnet on Value
http://www.LoveSystems.com/cd16

Braddock and Dahunter on Teasing
http://www.LoveSystems.com/cd30

Cajun and Tenmagnet on Role Plays
http://www.LoveSystems.com/cd32

Qualification:

Sinn and Vision on Qualification
http://www.LoveSystems.com/cd8

Mr. M, Bradock, and Sphinx on Issues in Qualification
http://www.LoveSystems.com/cd33

Seduction:

Sinn and Tenmagnet on Seduction
http://www.LoveSystems.com/cd12

Soul and Johnny Wolf on Logistics: Taking Her Home
http://www.LoveSystems.com/cd33

Relationships:

Relationship Management DVDs from Savoy
http://www.LoveSystems.com/Relationship-Management

Meeting women in bars & clubs:

Savoy and The Don on Advanced Winging
http://www.LoveSystems.com/cd21

Moxie and Future on Obstacles and Other Men
http://www.LoveSystems.com/cd7

Savoy and The Don on Cold Reads
http://www.LoveSystems.com/cd23

Mr. M and Sheriff on High-End Club Game
http://www.LoveSystems.com/cd26

Meeting women outside of bars and clubs:

Savoy and Tenmagnet on Warm Approach

http://www.LoveSystems.com/cd13

Savoy and Badboy on Social Circles
http://www.LoveSystems.com/cd20

Daytime Dating Workshop
http://www.LoveSystems.com/DayGame

Social Circle Mastery Seminar
http://www.LoveSystems.com/Social-Circle

Humor:

Sinn and Future on Storytelling
http://www.LoveSystems.com/cd3

Braddock and Cajun on Humor
http://www.LoveSystems.com/cd35

Humor, Improv, Attraction Seminar with Big Business
http://www.LoveSystems.com/training-programs/humor-improv-attraction

Mainstream humor books and DVDs that have been recommended by past students:

Humor Theory: Formula of Laughter by Igor Krichtafovitch

True and False: Heresy and Common Sense for the Actor by David Mamet

Three Uses of the Knife by David Mamet

Comedian (movie) by Jerry Seinfeld

Female Psychology:

Savoy and Soul on Female Psychology
http://www.LoveSystems.com/cd34

Phone Game:

Sinn and Savoy on Phone Game
http://www.LoveSystems.com/cd10

Dates:

Ajax and Future on Dates
http://www.LoveSystems.com/cd4

Fashion and Identity:

Tenmagnet, and Future on Identity
http://www.LoveSystems.com/cd6

Moxie and Savoy on Being In State
http://www.LoveSystems.com/cd29

Big Business and Prestige on Love Systems in Everyday Life
http://www.LoveSystems.com/cd36

Inner Game Seminar
http://www.LoveSystems.com/Inner-Game

Advanced Strategies – Important:

Sinn and Savoy on Frame Control
http://www.LoveSystems.com/cd5

Savoy and Brad P. on Taking Chances
http://www.LoveSystems.com/cd15

Sinn and The Don on Physical Progression and Kissing
http://www.LoveSystems.com/cd11

Savoy and Speer on Damage Control
http://www.LoveSystems.com/cd22

The Don and Savoy on Using and Creating Routines
http://www.LoveSystems.com/cd9

Tenmagnet, Braddock, and Cajun on Jealousy Plotlines
http://www.LoveSystems.com/cd24

Braddock, Mr. M, and Sheriff on How to Be an Alpha Male
http://www.LoveSystems.com/cd25

Soul, Badboy, and Cortez on Direct Game
http://www.LoveSystems.com/cd26

Braddock and Mr. M on 9 and 10 Game
http://www.LoveSystems.com/cd31

One Night Stands:

One Night Stands Seminar
http://www.LoveSystems.com/ons

Threesomes:

Savoy and Badboy on Threesomes
http://www.LoveSystems.com/cd18

Strippers and Hired Guns:

Strippers and Hired Guns Seminar
http://www.LoveSystems.com/Strippers

Interview Series Bundle Packs:

You can now pick up past Interview Volumes at amazingly discounted prices. Each Pack includes 10 volumes!

Interview Series Bundle Pack 1 (including Volumes 1-10)
http://www.LoveSystems.com/audio/interview-series-bundle-pack-1

Interview Series Bundle Pack 2 (including Volumes 11-20)
http://www.LoveSystems.com/audio/interview-series-bundle-pack-2

Interview Series Bundle Pack 3 (including Volumes 21-30)
http://www.LoveSystems.com/audio/interview-series-bundle-pack-3

Interview Series Bundle Pack 4 (including Volumes 31-40)

http://www.LoveSystems.com/audio/interview-series-bundle-pack-4

Interview Series Bundle Pack 5 (including Volumes 41-50)

http://www.LoveSystems.com/audio/interview-series-bundle-pack-5

Keep up to date

The best way to keep up to date with new developments in dating science is of course to subscribe to the Interview Series (http://www.LoveSystems.com/ivs). But that's not the only source of continuing information and resources. In fact, there are three good places to check out.

1. The Attraction Forums (http://www.theattractionforums.com). This phenomenal website is a great place to find a "wingman," to search for and read articles and "field reports" from the masters, to share information and ask questions to others, to find or post routines, and to make friends. It's free.
2. The Life With Soul blog (http://www.lifewithsoul.com). This is where Soul posts his thoughts on day game, women, love, and sex. You can find all of his classic articles and videos here and leave comments or get in touch with him.
3. The famous and complete Love Systems Publications Library (http://www.LoveSystems.com/publications). Many of the best techniques and field reports are added to this library, which grows every week. It's a great database for the best tips to develop your skills.

You will also want to check out our free newsletter, the Love Systems Insider (LSi). It's full of great information and new breakthroughs, and reading it regularly will inspire you to keep developing your skills. You can join (for free!) at the signup box on our homepage or go directly to (http://www.LoveSystems.com/LSi).

Conclusion

Not every good resource is listed here. However, this should give you a road map for the next year or so. We were once in your shoes, so we know what it's like. Write us any time at info@lovesystems.com.

Testimonials

This book is a great tool, and will provide you with a strong foundation for improving your skills and bolstering your confidence with women. With the knowledge gleaned from these pages and lots of practice, you will see a marked improvement in your interactions with women.

"When I met you on the workshop, I could see it in you. I could see that this guy can make a girl comfortable to sleep with him within minutes."

- *K. S., London*

"As she left, while I was coming in, I could sense joy radiating from her eyes. She was truly happy. This weekend has taught me so much: about life, about women, about myself, and most importantly has served to change people's lives for the better. It was the most intense emotional rollercoaster I've experienced since I started out."

- *Iena, London*

"I cannot find words to describe Soul. This guy is just passionate about what he does and cares about his students. I know it has been mentioned before but Soul exudes a charm that even James Bond and Casanova cannot emulate. He is the embodiment of confidence and smoothness."

- *Member of the Attraction Forums*

"I am new to the Love Systems community. I came here because I was in an abusive relationship. The guy beat me everyday and I did not have the confidence to leave. After reading Souls Inspire Others To Be Better post I felt I owed it to my kids to leave. Thank you Soul. I owe you."

- *Female member of the Attraction Forums*

"A friend of mine showed me the articles Stop Hanging Out With Unsuccessful People and Inspire Others To Be Better. Then I researched more of Soul. Since then I have had the confidence to leave my boyfriend of three years, who never had a job and lived off me completely. Soul is more than a life coach, he is a lifesaver."

- Molly, Kansas

"Think about the freedom you would feel if you could see a girl that you are genuinely interested in, approach her, have a great conversation, and create SERIOUS attraction whenever and wherever you want. The first step to getting to this point is to meet Soul."

- John D., Member of the Attraction Forums

"Jeremy is probably one of the best instructors I have ever met and I am not just referring to GAME (and I have been in post-secondary education for over 9 years). Jeremy is articulate, humble, passionate, and extremely supportive of his students. Moreover, the material he presents is invaluable."

- L.H., San Francisco

"There is no price tag on something that changes your life."

- S.S, Member of the Attraction Forums

"Out of all the instructors I've met Soul is the most truly driven by what he does, and he really does believe in improving the lives of the men that he coaches and the women that they inevitably end up in relationships with. He is also incredibly compassionate and understanding, and took the time to work with each of us not only on our game, but on the other things happening in our lives as well."

- Aaron S., Stockholm

"Jeremy is a great inspiration, genuine, a cool guy and an excellent teacher."

- J.B., Sydney

"Soul does a phenomenal job of relaying his great conversational skills to his students through his revolutionary concept of Mastery Topics. This completely changed the way I think of not only Day Game, but every single conversation I have from now on."

- B.M., Los Angeles

"Every single day since the seminar has been better than the last. Soul has finally pushed me over the edge, and has gotten me to face my fears and finally find a form of approach that's totally up my alley."

- S.C., New York City

"Soul's very good at what he does. He really has perfected the art of Day Game... you can tell from his mastery of the concepts that they are self-developed, and not just inherited and rehashed. Soul's Day Game is the best out there and somewhat refreshing for those tired of night game."

- B.J., New York City

"What I really admired about Soul's modus operandi is that it's rooted in authenticity. He's teaching you to be direct, open and honest to attract women rather than to manipulate them into liking you. So you won't be required to learn a long list of lines and stories and forced "cocky funny" banter. Soul's also a fantastic teacher - enthusiastic, highly articulate, and amusing and an expert (probably THE expert) in his day-game field – and a great bloke."

- S.D., London

"Soul is an excellent teacher, and his method is downright practical. I don't know how well Soul thinks he is accomplishing his objective, so I'll say it right now: He has hit the mark dead on. I'm familiar with the writings of numerous well-known methods, especially those written for day game. Soul's method is simply more specific, more practical, and more natural, than the others I've seen.... I am soooo happy that I took this class. It was life-changing for me. I feel so empowered. I wish every guy could experience what I did that weekend. It changed my life."

- S.N., San Francisco

"Soul taught everything so well, so well explained. He conveyed everything as simply as possible, so everyone could understand. It was methodical, and flowed with ease. From keys to success, inner game, to the Triad; to the whole emotional progression model in regards to Day Game, each step of the model -- all in depth with unbelievable detail. I loved it so much. Soul is just such an amazing teacher."

- K.B. London

"Then there was Soul. Sir you have changed my game completely once again. In all honesty, right now I almost feel like I've started down the road all over again, but this time I can see it is the right road to be on."

- Jim, New York City

"After the Day Game Workshop, I felt something changed in me. I felt way better about myself. I felt I have more control over my life. I felt that I can be somebody who I always wanted to be: an alpha male nice guy. Thank you Soul! The next time we meet and you ask me, "What is the last thing I wanted to do, but never did, and have regrets about", I would like to have the same answer as yours. Nothing."

- P.M., Los Angeles

"My first impression of Soul was of a fairly humble, unassuming, and yet confident guy-where was the star 'guru' pickup whirlwind of fury?! Refreshingly, not here! Soul is not a self-seeking 'guru'- he is there to help you succeed with dating women. Period. Ultimately, my experience of this program was nothing short of amazing, and Soul is the real deal- professional, empathetic, and totally passionate about helping guys achieve their dating dreams."

- F.N., Sydney

"From Soul I was given a real belief that you can meet women without needing to be a dancing monkey, without needing alcohol or to be in a nightclub, without needing to share a career, hobby or a mutual friend to introduce you and without needing to beat about the bush trying to be their friend first."

- B.B., Austin

"Soul's a very bright, pleasant, dedicated professional who is easy to get along with who will put you at ease instantly; within a few moments you will know instinctively that you've put yourself and your future in the right hands. He really does care about his students' progress and puts his soul (pun intended) into it. Although he's taught hundreds of boot camps and thousands of students at no time did I ever feel that I was getting a robotic response, but rather precisely what I needed at that moment, in that specific situation."

- Paul, New York City

"All in all I believe Soul is an exceptional trainer and coach... his method of sharing information makes complex material very easy to understand... he truly believes in what he teaches and is very passionate about it ... he has his heart into it when he teaches and it shows that he cares greatly about his students..."

- T.G., Oslo

"Other than being the best day game instructor I believe Soul is an exceptional human being... Thank you for everything Soul."

- Member of the Attraction Forums

"All I can say is that we all owe Soul a lot. The look of happiness and change in the students were just amazing. Soul's method will be the best method to improve your success with women you meet during the day time for a very long time to come. "

- S.B., New York City

"Soul sees body language and behavioral traits that offer him thinly sliced moments of memory recognition in, I guess, just about everyone. Perhaps this is why he is such a great instructor, with a legendary ability to find your flaws and help you fix them. He is all of Game. Not just Day. He is Night too. He is inner game, he has shown me a process in which I can approach, open, attract, qualify, validate, comfort, seduce, love and logistically escalate in two minutes flat with just one well constructed thoughtful but genuine interaction in which I can display the very best, most seductive version of myself to only those I am truly attracted to with little more than the most gentle and subtle of physical contact."

- B.K. Toronto

Congratulations on investing in Daytime Dating: Never Sleep Alone by Jeremy Soul! To download your exclusive bonus chapter on Conquering Approach Anxiety, click here:

www.LoveSystems.com/daytimedatingbonusdownload

Room for your notes